Acclaim for

IN TUNE

"Richard Wolf uniquely shows how the combination
of music and silence can be a doorway into the life-
changing benefits of a mindfulness practice."
—**Allen Weiss**, director of Mindful USC

"Not since Ram Dass's *Be Here Now* has a Western writer
truly examined the relationship between meditation and art as
Richard Wolf does in *In Tune*. As a frequent guest participant
in Richard's USC Music and Mindfulness lecture series, I have
seen firsthand the benefit of his unique approach to helping
young musicians achieve their potential through the practice of
artful listening and a relaxed, unfiltered awareness."
—**Clyde Lieberman**, Emmy Award–winning producer of *The Voice*

"Music has always been used by people in all different
cultures to consciously or unconsciously alter moods,
bring energy into the system, and, more importantly,
to lift oneself out of the limitations of one's ego. In this
book, Richard Wolf reveals the inner workings of the
transformational power of music and guides us further on
the path of living in this world in a harmonious way."
—**Krishna Das**, internationally acclaimed chant leader

"The excellent mindful meditation techniques that Richard Wolf teaches in this book, especially those centered on deep listening and tonal breathing, have been really helpful in unblocking my creativity. Thanks to Wolf's artful explanations and pointers, I've also been better focused and inspired to practice meditation."
—**Pete Scaturro**, senior music producer, Sony PlayStation

"I found nuggets in the book that I relate to, that I can work with, and that help me greatly with my practice. For instance, I've been counting bars my whole life. It's so connected that I don't remember how it started—it's become an intuitive thing from the music. Wolf's methods incorporating musical and rhythmic counting pick up on this—and have become my favorite ways to meditate."
—**Stephan M. Rowe**, music editor, *NCIS*

"It seems like everybody is talking about 'mindfulness' these days, but Richard Wolf uniquely connects that practice to the satisfaction and uplift we humans find in music. Whether you're someone capable of writing symphonies or someone who merely hums along to the radio, *In Tune* can help lead you to inner peace, personal insight, and greater productivity."
—**Chuck Crisafulli**, author of *Nirvana: Behind Every Song*

IN
TUNE

MUSIC AS THE BRIDGE
TO MINDFULNESS

How You Can Build a Lifelong Meditation
Practice through Sound—and Silence

RICHARD WOLF

THE EXPERIMENT

NEW YORK

The Experiment, LLC
220 East 23rd Street, Suite 600, New York, NY 10010-4658
theexperimentpublishing.com

Many of the designations used by manufacturers and sellers to distinguish their products are claimed as trademarks. Where those designations appear in this book and The Experiment was aware of a trademark claim, the designations have been capitalized.

The Experiment's books are available at special discounts when purchased in bulk for premiums and sales promotions as well as for fund-raising or educational use. For details, contact us at info@theexperimentpublishing.com.

Library of Congress Cataloging-in-Publication Data

Names: Wolf, Richard (Richard Lawrence), 1950- author.
Title: In tune : music as the bridge to mindfulness : how you can build a lifelong meditation practice through sound and silence / Richard Wolf.
Description: New York, NY : The Experiment, [2019]
Identifiers: LCCN 2018047853 | ISBN 9781615195350 (cloth)
Subjects: LCSH: Music--Psychological aspects. | Meditation.
Classification: LCC ML3830 .W64 2019 | DDC 781.1/1--dc23 LC record available at https://lccn.loc.gov/2018047853

ISBN 978-1-61519-535-0
Ebook ISBN 978-1-61519-536-7

Cover design by Sarah Smith | Text design by Beth Bugler
Author photograph by James Pratt

Manufactured in China

First printing April 2019
10 9 8 7 6 5 4 3 2 1

In Tune is dedicated to my parents, Jacques and Charlotte Wolf, who taught me to listen with sympathetic resonance to the players in the orchestra and the silent stirrings of the heart.

"Before transmitting the music in your soul, help others hear the music in theirs."

—Seeds of Wisdom

CONTENTS

Preludes to
Practice

Hearing Something Different

FROM THE TIME I WAS seventeen I'd been engaged in an on-again, and mostly off-again, affair with meditation. There was a Zen center around the corner from the apartment I grew up in, on Eighty-First Street and West End Avenue in Manhattan. I was a senior in high school when I first had my curiosity piqued by books about Zen by Dr. D. T. Suzuki, Philip Kapleau, and Alan Watts. These writers had attained some visibility in the counterculture, and they struck a chord in me. So I started to practice zazen (Zen meditation) under the guidance of the very strict Japanese master at the center. I continued meditating during my freshman year in college, and for the next three decades I dipped in and out of my practice in phases that always ended in despair. I was unable to reach enlightenment or master the method of quieting my uncooperative mind; no sooner was I was emboldened by a few days of relative tranquility than I hit a patch of turbulence in my life that would throw me completely off course.

And then there was the physical pain. The zazen that I learned included only two posture variations, either sitting on your knees or sitting cross-legged yoga-style on the floor. Since my body bends about as much as a fluted pilaster, all the positions were painful; often I found myself focusing on the extreme discomfort instead of on the proper object of concentration (usually the breath). And in the rare moments when my focus was unshackled from the physical pain, my mind would gleefully bolt in any random direction. I told myself that meditation was too hard, and I just wasn't cut out for it.

Until one day I had a sudden realization. It led me to make a quantum leap from one practice that I engaged with all my life, to a second practice with which I had struggled for much of my life.

The first was music. My mother was a gifted pianist, my father played drums in jazz combos in his youth, and both are dedicated and erudite music aficionados. I started writing songs when I was five, and my parents enrolled me in piano lessons when I was six. Since college I've been involved with music on a professional level: producing, songwriting, composing, remixing, and arranging the music on records, films, and television shows. I've had my share of career setbacks and disappointments, but in general it's been a lucky and upbeat trajectory. The victories overall have outweighed and outlasted the defeats.

But for a period of time, the combined pressures of family responsibilities and TV deadlines had me spelunking down a cavernous anxiety hole. And it all came to a head one night when I was rushed to the ER because my heart decided to shuffle like Muhammad Ali and box its way out of my chest. Soon thereafter, I sought help. My panic and anxiety clinical therapist prescribed twenty minutes of meditation a day, ten minutes in the morning and ten at night. When I asked him to show me what meditation method he recommended, he replied that he wasn't a meditation teacher so couldn't give a suggestion. However, he offered something of a demonstration by leaning back comfortably in his chair and closing his eyes. He told me to sit like that and stay calm. That session taught me a major lesson that launched the new phase—a successful return to meditation—because now I saw that I didn't have to torture myself with contortions on the floor to meditate. If you are relatively inflexible and not used to sitting on the floor, you don't have to. The session reawakened the gravitational pull that meditation practice had been exerting on me since my teen years.

But the real epiphany came soon thereafter. One day on a business trip to New York, I was between meetings at the ABC offices near Lincoln Center, and I had an hour to kill. So I ended up at the huge Barnes & Noble down the street, where I happened upon a book by a distinguished Tibetan meditation teacher, *Turning the Mind into an Ally* by Sakyong Mipham. Drawing on his experience working with horses and falcons, he compared the taming of these animals to training the "wild mind." He wrote that just as the trainer has to gently lead the horse back to the path if it stumbles or strays, so the meditator needs to lead the wandering mind back to the one point of concentration.

Of course this wasn't the first time an author or teacher recommended that a wandering mind should be gently brought back to the center of attention. There had been many voices advising that the distracted mind or "monkey mind" could gradually be trained with the proper patience and softness. Yes, I had heard that refrain before; but this time I heard something different. Maybe because my earnestness to relieve my anxiety opened me to it, and in that space the message could finally sink in.

In the past when my mind wandered, at some point I just gave up. I thought that maybe these professional meditators could train their minds, but I couldn't train mine. What was different this time was that I made a connection to my first practice: music. I realized that when I wanted to play a piano piece, I just practiced it doggedly until I could play it better. I trained my fingers like Mr. Mipham trained his horse. I persevered because I believed that with enough time, effort, and patience, my fingers would eventually cooperate. So I realized that, maybe, practicing meditation is like practicing an instrument. Practice is practice! If I can do one, I can do the other. I always knew that I was way short of the talent it would take to be a really good piano (or guitar, or any other instrument) player: I was light-years away from even being in the same galaxy as McCoy Tyner or Herbie Hancock, some of my musical idols. Yet with my mediocre abilities I had already experienced the benefits of practice in the musical domain. That was enough proof to encourage me to think that practice would work in the contemplative realm as well.

Anyone, across the entire talent spectrum, who has ever trained to play an instrument—including the vocal instrument—knows that practice is necessary in order to advance. When you confront a difficult passage in music, the way to get through it is to go over it again and again, ideally with calm resolve. You *concentrate* on playing it through. And when you stumble over a difficult passage you don't despair, you just play it slowly again. And again. You train your fingers to play it, and you gradually get better. That's the nature of practice.

Why not transfer the same habits and abilities from practicing an instrument to practicing meditation? Instead of despairing when you're stuck in a difficult train of thought or worry, why not trust that the wandering mind is just like fumbled fingering on the piano—a natural part of the process? With practice it gets easier. And practice requires a daily commitment, which is something you eventually enjoy and look forward to.

But it's not just musical practice that lends itself to meditation. In fact, anyone who participates in an endeavor that requires training or practice, especially involving harmony between mind and body (for example, boxing, dancing, football, or gymnastics), can transfer these abilities and experiences to practicing meditation. If it requires continued dedicated periods of repetition, drills, concentration, trust, and dedication, it's an activity that develops skills and conditioning that can be applied to meditation. Practice is practice is practice.

Once I made the leap from musical practice to meditative mindfulness practice, many other connections between the two activities revealed themselves. Of course they both require perseverance, trust, discipline, concentration, repetition, and patience—qualities we'll explore more in this book. But music also cultivates our innate ability to listen carefully and deeply, a skill that's also a principle technique for the cultivation of mindfulness. In music the intuitive aspect of consciousness is tapped, nurtured, and encouraged; the same is true in contemplative practice. And harmonizing body and mind, feeling and intellect, so that they vibrate in perfect unison is at the heart of both practices.

Of course there are differences between music and meditation, and they are important, but the common ground between the two practices can lay a solid foundation for enhancing both endeavors. This realization set me on my current path toward a consistently beneficial and calming practice. Hopefully this book can ease the way for you to begin or maintain your own practice. Music can be a bridge between body and mind, the primitive and refined, the material and immaterial. And it can also be a bridge to a more expansive awareness and a more harmonious way of life.

The Fruits of Mindfulness

The words *medicine* and *meditation* are both rooted in the Latin *mederi*, which means "to heal." Healing is a good place to start when talking about the many benign attributes of mindfulness and meditation.

Probably one reason that you've picked up this book is that you're aware of the growing body of evidence suggesting that mindful meditation can be very beneficial to your mental, physical, and emotional health. Research conducted at the University of Massachusetts Medical School shows that mindfulness meditation aids in lowering blood pressure, helps to relieve stress, increases the ability to focus, stabilizes mood, supports clearer decision-making and overall brain function, produces contentment and feelings of well-being, improves the immune system, and even minimizes pain sensitivity. And those are just the rewards that fall in the self-healing and improvement category. Many have attested to reaping some of mindfulness's potential social and moral benefits as well, such as increasing the capacity for compassion and loving-kindness and making it easier to listen to another person with understanding and patience. Finally, many have experienced transformative changes in consciousness that have led to a renewed sense of wonder and a heightened appreciation of life.

What do we mean by *mindfulness*, and what is meditation? Mindfulness can be described as knowing what is happening while it is happening. It is a clear, undistracted awareness of being where you are right now. Rather than reacting to circumstances, you can be more of a spectator, observing events calmly, without judgment or entanglement. Your responses can then be calibrated to be more reasoned and peaceful. Whatever transpires at the moment is apprehended directly without the constant static of your thoughts, conceptions, and emotions warping the present reality. And it's not just in your head—your whole being can embody a tranquil and stable state of relaxed and enhanced wakefulness. As Yogi Berra summed up, "You can observe a lot just by watching."

We all experience brief episodes of mindfulness in organic, unintentional ways. There can be minutes at a time while driving a car when we direct full, undistracted attention to myriad factors on the road. But to *practice* mindfulness as a life skill requires some basic training and exercises, as would be necessary in cultivating any other skill. Overwhelming testimony indicates that the most reliable training for developing mindfulness is meditation.

Meditation consists of two basic elements: *concentration* and *mindfulness*. (Some traditions include *insight* as a third element, but that can also be described as a natural product of the first two.) In concentration, we focus the busy and noisy mind in one direction. Then we gradually tune out the white noise from a multiplicity of signals by tuning in to the object of our focus, like a visual or a sound, even the sound of our own breathing. As the mind settles down, a quiet calm spreads throughout the body. We compose ourselves.

Concentration allows the energies of mind and body to be steady, whole, and unified. And that leads to a much clearer vision of what's going on. It's as if you were taking a video with your cell phone and notice that your hands are shaking with excitement. Unless you calm down and steady your grip, your video will turn out all jittery and blurry. You'll hardly be able to see a thing. However, once you are calm enough to stabilize the camera, you'll get a clear picture. Concentration leads to the composure of a steady mind, which then leads to greater clarity.

If concentration is the ability to focus in an undistracted manner on one object, *mindfulness* is the ability to focus in the same manner on whatever arises in your field of awareness. Some have even characterized mindfulness as concentration on serial objects or events rather than focused attention on one point. Once the mind is composed and stabilized through deep concentration, a relaxed, enhanced awareness can naturally evolve as your attention opens up to include whatever is happening in your experience at the moment. Having a strong foundation in concentration enables you to maintain your attention when you move your focus from one point in concentration to all points in mindfulness.

The composure and clarity that you find in these practices can lead to feelings of joy, peace, and contentment. Instead of straining yourself in the frantic pursuit of happiness, you're pausing long enough to actually *be* happy. You notice that being this calm, clear, and composed allows you to take in and fully savor the pure pleasures of peace.

And the pleasures of peace are not to be underestimated; it is no accident that in many cultures people say to each other, "May you go in peace," or, "May peace be upon you." In our culture when someone passes away we say, "May she rest in peace." But why wait until you're dead to rest in peace?

The Twelve Bridges Between Music and Mindfulness

"The mental concentration and physical stamina that
result from these [Tibetan meditative] disciplines is
virtually identical to that needed in music making and
performing. To this point, I can't even say which
comes first."—**Philip Glass, *Words Without Music***

Early in my musical career I noticed that some of the musicians
I admired most were reported to practice meditative disciplines:
Leonard Cohen, Paul McCartney, Carlos Santana, John Coltrane, Robert Plant, Tina Turner, Philip Glass, Herbie Hancock, Wayne Shorter—to mention only the most celebrated.
And over time the list expanded to include hip-hop luminaries
Rick Rubin, 50 Cent, J. Cole, and Kendrick Lamar. It seemed
that there must be some unique and mysterious wavelength
that could cause the separate fields of music and meditation to
vibrate in sympathetic attunement, but I couldn't find a satis-
factory explanation for those connections.

Once I realized that confidence in the payoff of practice could
be a fundamental link bridging music with mindfulness, other
such bridges came to light. As my practice started to fall into a
steady rhythm, it became apparent that many skills and habits
developed through musical practice are transferable to meditative mindfulness practice.

These conditions supporting music and mindfulness form a
vibrant ecosystem of mutually beneficial factors. Among them are

what I like to think of as twelve primary "bridges" between the practices: dedication, posture, concentration, harmony, practice for the sake of practice, the art of deep listening, patience and perseverance, mindfulness and creativity, trance, sympathetic vibrations, transcending the self, and silence. Each of these qualities reinforces the others; each is useful to both practices. And both disciplines experience the world primarily through nonverbal, highly intuitive, mentally and physically integrated states of transpersonal consciousness. These similarities help explain the strong natural affinity that musicians, including the ones I've admired, have had for meditation practice.

Fortunately, you don't have to be a professional musician for music to have implanted these meditative qualities in you. If at any time in your life you've ever taken up a musical instrument, done voice or dance training, or completely immersed yourself in deep listening, you have already cultivated many of these skills to some degree. Music has already tuned your headspace for mindfulness.

Music has already tuned your
headspace for mindfulness.

But more importantly, meditation and mindfulness are simpler and more democratic practices than music. Genetic gifts aren't necessary for mindfulness. You don't need natural talent to get to the mindfulness equivalent of a finish line or to ascend to the top of the meditation charts. For over two thousand years of contemplative traditions it has been generally accepted that anyone whose most basic needs for survival are met can meditate. According to Buddhism and other traditions, everyone is already meditating and inherently enlightened. They're just not yet aware of it.

Underscoring these connections, the classic meditation teachings of zazen, *pranayama* (from yoga), and *vipassana* (mindfulness or insight meditation) can be approached from an instinctively musical perspective. In these instructions we highlight modes of mindfulness that draw on ways of focusing and interacting with experience that are second nature for musical minds. These techniques are means of bridging the gap between music and mindfulness. To give just one example, all these traditions give the instruction to "follow" the breath. Sounds simple, but in fact sitting still without distraction and just concentrating on the breath is pretty hard to do. But it makes it easier to follow the breath by listening to the sound of the breath with a musician's ear. Your attention can be anchored in noticing subtle rhythmic, harmonic, and sonic characteristics of the music of life in the breath. And you can be highly sensitive to these unfolding characteristics while maintaining a clear detachment and without getting caught up in analysis or reactivity.

While meditating, it's equally important to attend to moments of silence with the same inquisitiveness and absorption with which you listen to the music of breathing. And when the field of awareness in meditation expands to take in everything that happens besides the breath, we listen in the same way. We experience the external and internal soundscapes with the same nonjudgmental attentiveness, still taking note of the play between sound and silence. Eventually this mindful exploration leads to our diving deep down beneath the surface of sound and silence to meet their source.

Being conscious of these harmonic convergences can build confidence in the process and ease the way to better focus, composure, peacefulness, and enhanced awareness. They can encourage the practice to flow into a life of its own.

The many bridges that connect the two disciplines can be helpful in creating the conditions for mindfulness to take root in your life. Being conscious of these harmonic convergences can build confidence in the process and ease the way to better focus, composure, peacefulness, and enhanced awareness. They can encourage the practice to flow into a life of its own.

In the following twelve chapters we will take a closer look at each of the bridges that support the special relationship between music and meditative mindfulness.

Changing Your Mind

It's hard to describe the (potentially) profound transformative effects of this practice without sounding immoderately effusive or trippy. But as Mark Twain said of Richard Wagner, "The music is better than it sounds." Just because you have this kind of practice doesn't mean you always walk around a few inches off the ground. Even longtime, skillful practitioners are challenged to maintain the kind of equanimity, tranquility, discernment, and composure described here. Mindfulness is hardly a one-size-fits-all miracle drug. Practice doesn't guarantee perfection, but if you put in the effort the odds are you'll experience some discernible improvement in performance and well-being.

Knowing that there is this spectrum of possible outcomes, from a little de-stressing to a full awakening, can keep a practitioner motivated on the path. Yet hearing this, some meditation purists may discordantly chime in that you're not supposed to want to achieve anything with this practice and there is really nothing to attain. Which ultimately is true: It's more a process of uncovering what you already have inside yourself than acquiring something out there. But if you don't believe that you have something to gain by the practice, why would you begin in the first place?

It's kind of like that anecdote about Niels Bohr and his lucky horseshoe. Bohr, the Nobel Prize–winning physicist and leading pioneer of quantum theory, was recognized as one of the greatest scientific minds of the twentieth century. One day a visitor noticed that he had a horseshoe hanging above his doorway and asked him about its purpose.

Bohr is reported to have responded, "It's said that hanging a horseshoe above the door brings good luck."

"But surely you don't believe in it?" the visitor asked incredulously.

"You don't have to believe in it in order for it to work," he replied.

Maybe you don't necessarily have to believe in it for mindfulness or meditation to work. But you do need to help it hang around like the horseshoe long enough to give it a chance to do its thing. If you do, you will likely start to notice a difference. It may even change your mind.

The Twelve Bridges

1.

Dedication

"Meditation is a must, it don't hurt if you try."
—Kendrick Lamar

MUSICIANS HAVE TO SET ASIDE time on a regular basis for learning and practice. Even amateur musicians dedicate some time during the week to take lessons and practice. Meditation practice also requires a small but not insignificant degree of dedication.

As opposed to most serious musical practice, meditation does not require a lot of time. Ten minutes a day is a common way to begin a practice. Whereas in music ten minutes won't get you too far, with meditation ten minutes will get you on your way to greater peace and clarity. Yet as with music, the longer your practice sessions, the likelier you are to make progress. So you gradually may want to extend your sitting to fifteen- and twenty-minute sessions to get more benefit.

Even once you've carved out the time to meditate, doing so consistently might present further obstacles. Meditation and mindfulness training are most effective when practiced on a regular basis—ideally daily. But budgeting the time in your busy schedule to squeeze in this new practice will be a challenge. It will require a level of resolve that can resist the constant demands on your attention. Luckily, thanks to music you already have some skill in this area. When starting out as a budding musician you recognized that you needed to carve out time in your day to practice. It's a reasonable guess that your dedication to learning your instrument helped you find a routine that allowed you to practice more or less consistently. Now you can call on that experience of setting aside distractions on a daily basis to help you progress in this new endeavor. Once you've resolved to make a serious effort to follow the path of mindfulness, applying the dedication and disciplined time management that you've already refined in music to this new practice should be natural.

Dedication is the first bridge because it is not only essential to building a daily practice, but it's also pretty much a foundation for everything that follows. No musician ever became moderately successful without being dedicated to making music. A strong resolve is necessary in overcoming the setbacks, failures, disappointments, and disillusionment that we all experience as musicians. Why would meditation practice be any different?

KEY STEPS IN YOUR PRACTICE:
CREATING THE CONDITIONS

"All of man's misfortunes derive from one thing, which
is not knowing how to sit still in a quiet room."
—**Blaise Pascal**

When starting out, creating the conditions for mindful meditation practice will help it take root in our lives. Then the practice happens by itself. Once the soil is prepared, the seed can flower. As Shunryu Suzuki said: "Never think that you are sitting zazen . . . zazen is sitting zazen."

What are some useful conditions for developing mindful meditation? It begins with the intention and commitment to practice. Having trust in the efficacy of practice and taking joy in the pleasures of peace are good foundations in the long term. Having confidence that the more you repeat the process, the more progress you eventually will make, is helpful. Finding joy in the pleasures of peace that meditation can bring is a strong but gentle motivator. And of course, the many links we've pointed to between musical practice and meditative mindfulness practice happily embody conditions that can nurture the practice.

Periodically immersing yourself

in the culture of calm attention can

tone down the effects of these

stress-producing circumstances.

One important way to support your practice is to continue to enrich your understanding of meditation and mindfulness by reading, listening to podcasts, or watching lectures in the field. In daily life you may constantly be faced with stressful situations, failure and disappointment, and looming storms on the horizon—not to mention an endless barrage of information and digital overload designed to tip your tenuous balance. Periodically immersing yourself in the culture of calm attention can tone down the effects of these stress-producing circumstances. And what you learn about mindfulness and meditation from the experience of others not only enhances your understanding of your own experience but also contributes to the conditions that will nurture your practice

TECHNIQUES: BUILDING A REPERTOIRE

Conscious breathing and deep listening are classic techniques in many meditation traditions, from zazen to Tibetan Buddhism, from yoga to vipassana (mindfulness meditation). I've adapted some of the proven methods and modified them to draw on the experiences, habits, and sensibilities of those who have had some musical training. By amplifying the musical potential within classic methods, we can make meditation and mindfulness training, which can be dry and difficult, more natural and pleasurable. The practitioner can engage with many of these exercises as both a path to heightened awareness and as an improvised performance in the act of composing oneself.

There's a saying that "one who controls the breath controls the mind." Most of the meditation techniques we will go into are based on this classic foundation of focusing on the breath. But there are many other methods that can be included in a full repertoire of techniques and that musically inclined people may be particularly attuned to. These methods easily cross over to general usefulness for anyone with a rudimentary sense of rhythm and tonality.

It may also be helpful to practice different concentration techniques at different times. Just as playing the same scale in the same key ad infinitum may be monotonous and just plain mind-numbing, practicing the same meditation method repetitively may lose effectiveness or appeal. The mind craves novelty and challenge, and it's fun to try out new and different meditation strategies depending on the day and the mood.

Sometimes I picture concentration on the breath as the laying down of a solid groove by a rhythm section. While the rhythm section keeps the beat, the lead instruments or voices can go off in infinite directions. Likewise, while attention to the qualities of the breath solidly establishes the focus of our awareness, we can then expand that field of focus to be all-inclusive of whatever is happening in our experience at that moment, and meet it with greater clarity and understanding.

Counting

Since counting to keep time is at the heart of music making, counting the breath can play an important role in some meditative techniques. There are various ways of counting the breath. In most of the classic meditation traditions, the inhalation and exhalation are counted as one breath. Most beginners assume that they should count "one" on the inhalation and "two" on the exhalation, and so forth. However, you'll find that in the methods discussed here, the inhalation and exhalation are mostly treated as one breath. Some practitioners repeat the number during both the in-breath and out-breath, while others prefer to count only during the exhalation.

I've heard different reasons for counting the in-breath and out-breath as one. Inhaling and exhaling are two different sides of the same one breath, so why not count it as such? But there are also larger ramifications to the two steps being treated as one. Our perceptions are normally mired in dualistic concepts, tending to perceive two different aspects of a single process as two separate and self-existent events. We discern the differences, which are real, but ignore the fact that these differences are two sides of one unity, as if the coin has a separate and independent front and a separate, independent back. That the in-breath and out-breath are two separate aspects of one unified process and need to be counted as such is representative of a universally nondualistic viewpoint.

Another factor to keep in mind is that you will eventually release yourself from the technique. Your intense, single-pointed concentration will yield to a widening of perception, to a sense of total receptivity. So if at some point you begin to experience a deep insight or realization, let yourself go. Stop counting and just let the experience happen. At this point you may gain a bit more clarity into an aspect of your non-ego self, your life, or the quality of your experience. Allow your field of consciousness to be limitless and take in whatever occurs at the moment. Then as it passes, let it go.

Filling Out the Repertoire

Every chapter for the rest of this book contains one or more meditation or mindfulness exercises, such as counting the breath. These techniques can form the foundation of your practice. But there may be times when making a few of your own adjustments to a method may yield more satisfying results. Having a broad repertoire of practice modes can be helpful over the long term because the mind craves novelty and challenge. Having a selection of alternative methods also gives you a lot of room to experiment. You may find that one or two methods seem to take you where you want to go and are just fine the way they are. At other times you may find yourself improvising with a familiar technique to keep going in a flow state. If you're inspired to get creative with a technique, go for it. Use the means that you find the most useful and give you the most joy. Be your own teacher.

If you're interested in experimenting with more musically technical exercises, please explore the "Bonus Tracks" section at the end of the book. Those exercises are a bit more complex and may be best suited for those with at least a basic acquaintance with the concept of intervals in music.

———

Be your own teacher.

———

TECHNIQUE: LET'S GET STARTED

Let's get started with our first meditation.

First, set a timer for the amount of time you want to meditate. This way you won't be constantly checking to see how long you've been sitting. Let's begin with ten minutes.

Find a quiet spot where you can sit without being disturbed. If you're sitting in a chair, make sure your feet are positioned so that your body is supported well enough that you can sit comfortably with a relatively upright back. If you can sit without leaning on the back of the chair, that's preferable. If you're sitting on the floor, the "half lotus" or "quarter lotus" positions are recommended. You can use the zazen technique of moving your trunk in gradually narrowing circles until you feel balanced and centered. A flexible but strong posture is always desirable, as it not only helps concentration but also affords the lungs, diaphragm, and abdomen maximum room to maneuver. Striking the balance between calm relaxation and energetic attention in the body and mind can be compared to tuning a stringed instrument. If the strings are too loose, they will not have the necessary tonality. If they are tuned too tightly, they will break.

Striking the balance between calm
relaxation and energetic attention in
the body and mind can be compared
to tuning a stringed instrument. If the
strings are too loose, they will not have
the necessary tonality. If they are tuned
too tightly, they will break.

Either close your eyes or fix your gaze softly a few feet in front of you at approximately a forty-five-degree downward angle. It's better (but not necessary) to keep the eyes cast down and half-closed with a soft focus, because doing so is more conducive to wakefulness. Many practitioners use candles, stones, or other objects to help keep their gaze steady and attention focused. Place your hands on your lap, resting them palms-down and just above your knees. The chin should be gently tucked in so it's level with the floor. Place the tongue near the roof of the mouth, just touching the two front teeth.

If you are able to inhale and exhale exclusively through your nose without any hindrance, do so. If this causes any discomfort, try to inhale through the nose and exhale through the mouth.

Relax your shoulders, your arms, your hands. With every exhalation, relax a different part of your body. Notice if there is any tension anywhere and ease it. You are aware that you are breathing with your whole body. You can feel your whole body involved in breathing.

There are two basic ways to anchor your attention to the breath: by following the bodily movements and sensations and by listening deeply to the sound of your breathing. As you inhale, expand your abdomen and lift your diaphragm to make room for the air; as you exhale, bring in your abdomen, so that your chest falls as your lungs empty. Think of an accordion: When you stretch the bellows the air flows in, and when you contract the instrument the air escapes. Air and music flow in both directions.

This is a musician's guide, so audio-centric methods are a natural fit. As you maintain awareness of the body you can also follow the breath by practicing the art of listening. Just as when you play an instrument or sing, your attention is both on your bodily movements and on listening to the music you are making, so here also you have these dual anchors of attention—your bodily movements and the sound of your breath.

Breathe in and out through the nose, and make your breathing strong enough so that it's audible. Listen to the sound of your breathing as if you are listening to the sound of music. The sound of your own breathing is a beautiful sound; it's the sound of your life.

The sound of your own

breathing is a beautiful sound;

it's the sound of your life.

Now add counting the breaths as you listen. As we noted earlier, a complete cycle of inhalation and exhalation is counted as one breath. There are various methods of counting but we begin by counting on the exhalation. You can count from one to ten. If you lose count, return to one again. When you find that your concentration wanders, don't get disheartened; just bring your attention gently back to the breath. When you flub the notes in a difficult musical passage that you are trying to master, you don't despair; you just play it again, this time more slowly. And again. You train your fingers to play it, and it gradually gets better. In the same way, repeatedly pulling the distracted attention back to the object of concentration will strengthen your concentrative muscles. The roaming mind is natural and to be expected. Every time you notice that your focus has drifted and you nudge your attention back on track, you are doing the work of meditation.

One more very significant tip: A major theme of the methods within this guide is to take the art of listening one important step further. We use the same intense focus on listening to the pauses in between the breaths as we use when listening to the breaths themselves—like the rests in music, which are necessary pauses in composition. Try to pause in between the inhalation-exhalation cycles. At the end of an inhalation, briefly hold your breath and "rest." Listen to the silence. You are still. Then exhale. At the end of the exhalation, as the last bit of air trickles out and your body is still again, stop and listen. Listen attentively to the sounds of these silent moments as your abdomen contracts and the body rests. You can stop and listen either between inhalations and exhalations, between exhalations and inhalations, or both. These stretches of silence are fertile fields for cultivating awareness and insight. The more you meditate, the more you will plow the pauses between the restless sounds of your thoughts.

2.

Posture

WHEN WE PLAY AN INSTRUMENT, we are aware of our body's relationship to the instrument. We are using our body to invite sound from the instrument by plucking, hitting, blowing, bowing, strumming, picking, striking, vocalizing, and so on. Musicians are very aware of the position of their bodies while performing on their instruments, and each instrument requires something different. As a pianist, I was always taught the importance of maintaining a particular posture at the edge of the piano bench. We take posture for granted, but think how awkward it would be for a concert pianist to play while straddling a dining room chair or a singer to record in a reclining position (unless the musician is using the unorthodox positioning to make a deliberate artistic statement or unique sound).

Posture in meditation, as in musical performance, is extremely important. We are trying to support our bodies to maintain focused attention while at the same time staying relaxed. Just as our goal mentally is to achieve relaxed awareness—a calm but clear and attentive state of mind—physically we adapt a posture to support that balanced and flexible state.

Just as our goal mentally is to achieve relaxed awareness—a calm but clear and attentive state of mind—physically we adapt a posture to support that balanced and flexible state.

Think of a soldier standing in a line in front of a drill sergeant. First the sergeant commands the soldier to "attention" and the soldier stands rigidly erect, stable, motionless, and alert. Then the sergeant commands his soldier to be "at ease." The soldier loosens up, separates his feet, and relaxes his shoulders, legs, and arms. Meditation posture combines both "attention" and "at ease" into one posture. This sounds paradoxical and maybe even impossible, but it is actually fairly intuitive and is achievable by anyone. We know from tuning stringed instruments that finding the right proportion of tension and relaxation achieves the desired pitch. The same balance of relaxation and focus is mirrored in the state of mental equilibrium achieved during meditation. We seek a posture that allows us to sustain a high degree of alert concentration while at the same time relaxing into awareness and thereby being freed of the stresses and pressures that can interfere with a clear and stable mind.

KEY STEPS IN YOUR PRACTICE:
SCHEDULING TIME

Just as consistent, daily training is key to learning an instrument, the same holds true for meditation practice. Find a time during your day that is most conducive to practicing. There are many theories as to what time is best, but one size doesn't fit all. Some people like to meditate first thing in the morning when their minds are fresh, before the stress has had time to pile up; others prefer sitting before going to bed. Others find time during lunch or at work before the day gets into full gear.

It's important to stick to your schedule once you find the optimum time for your practice. Try not to miss a day. Even if you have only a few minutes in a particular day to set aside for meditation, and even if it's not your "usual" time for sitting, make use of those few minutes. Just stop, rest, and be mindful of your being in the present moment.

It's generally thought among most traditions that meditating between twenty and thirty minutes will sustain a daily practice. But if you can set aside only ten minutes a day, even five, to practice, you will be heartened to know that many have found this to be ample time to begin a basic practice.

If you are just beginning, start slow: Try five to ten minutes a day, gradually working up to twenty minutes. Once you're able to sit with a good degree of stability and calmness for twenty minutes, you will probably want to sit for longer periods of time.

Feel free to experiment with longer sessions. There may also be opportunities, such as during a weekly "Day of Mindfulness" or during a retreat, when you will be encouraged to sit for multiple sessions for longer periods.

There are some traditions that recommend practicing twice a day. If you are just beginning and can sit for only ten minutes at a time, it may be helpful to try to sit for two sessions of ten minutes each. On the other hand, more advanced practitioners can practice twice daily for twenty minutes or vary the durations of their two sittings with different combinations of sitting times.

TECHNIQUE: TUNING THE DRUM

"Get Loose"—**Prince**

We can put the kind of body awareness that we maintain as musicians to very practical use while meditating. At the beginning of your meditation session, after you're settled into a comfortable position, it's useful practice to "tune the drum." This is when you focus on different sensations and parts of your body while also being mindful of your breathing.

Imagine your body is a huge drum. Before you can play the drum, you need to tune it. We begin by loosening the skin of the drum on all sides. This will give the drum a deep tone, a profound frequency with a long wavelength that will travel far. At the same time, you don't want to have too much slackness, which might lead you to lose the desired tonality. But if you tune it too tightly, it won't produce a satisfying sound. As with tuning any instrument, it's a matter of finding the right balance.

This applies to tuning both the body and the mind. Mentally, you want to balance relaxation with attentiveness. Physically, you loosen every part of your body where you may feel stress, from head to toe, just like loosening the skin of the drum. Even as you release tension in different areas of the body, you stay mindful of your posture as stable and supple. We can still locate and relax various stresses and tensions in the body while maintaining a balanced and flexible posture.

A relaxed body then helps calm the mind.

Here, the goal is to "get loose." The energy spent on remembering and thinking about all your concerns and desires keeps the body high strung, in constant tension. The physical stress then feeds back to amplify the tautness of the mind. Conversely, we can pause and consciously loosen the tension in the body. A relaxed body then helps calm the mind. Meditation practice leads to a sense of equanimity and clarity by relaxing body and mind together, loosening the grip of constricting concepts, notions, and conditioning.

Here's a practice for "tuning the drum":

Scan the different parts of your body with the goal of loosening any tense areas. You also want to bring calm awareness to the different parts of your body in general. Include all your internal organs, starting with your eyes, tongue, ears, and teeth, as well as your muscles from head to toe. Relax the muscles around your eyes, in your cheeks, around your lips. (You'll notice that when you relax the muscles around your mouth, your lips may turn into a slight half smile, like the ones you see on images of the Buddha.) If you feel tightness anywhere, use your awareness to guide your breath to that area and loosen it up. In addition to awareness of discomfort or tension, be conscious of your body's position in general. Be aware of where a part of your body may be touching another object or body part: your feet on the floor, buttocks on the chair, hands in your lap, and so on. Let go as much as possible while staying in tune; let gravity do the work of keeping your feet on the floor, hands on your lap, and so on.

Reside now in the place in which you experience

your awareness, wherever that may be.

. . .

We can resonate with what enables us to

be here, to breathe, and to have this awareness

of breathing and living.

Once you've attended to the different parts of your body with your awareness, try to locate where that awareness lives. Various cultures locate the seat of consciousness in different places. Some hold that consciousness has no central location but is spread expansively within the whole body. Reside now in the place in which you experience your awareness, wherever that may be.

Spend at least the first few minutes of every session this way. As your session progresses, when you feel attention wavering, return to connecting to your body. Your mind may wander elsewhere but your body is always right here, right now. Continue letting go of any tension, relieving stress, loosening stiffness, and tuning the drum to a rich, deep pitch. Attuned this way, we can begin to move toward harmony. We can resonate with what enables us to be here, to breathe, and to have this awareness of breathing and living.

TECHNIQUE: LISTENING MEDITATION— COUNTING SILENCE

Music lovers are acute listeners. We are used to discerning a multiplicity of factors in a passage of music: timbres, textures, harmonies, emotions, rhythms, melodies, pitches, and sonics. When we listen to silence we can use the same intense focus and one-pointed awareness that we use when we listen to music.

A helpful technique may be to count the silences. Instead of counting breaths, count the rest at the end of the exhalation. Say the number silently and then listen. Then resume your next inhalation. Count the silences from one to ten, then back down to one. Pause at the bottom. If you feel you can continue to breathe and count in this manner for the duration of your meditation session, do so. Otherwise, just breathe normally but continue to listen deeply to the silence between breaths. If you feel your attention drifting, resume counting the silences. Remember to be wise whenever holding the breath; hold it only for as long as it feels natural and comfortable.

Mindfully following the alternating rhythm of sound and silence can flow into an experience of profound stillness and calm clarity.

The more you meditate, the more you will hear the silences between the restless static of your thoughts. It usually takes a while, but with practice the silences between thoughts will get longer. With longer silences you may enjoy a new peace and spaciousness in the field of your awareness. Mindfully following the alternating rhythm of sound and silence can flow into an experience of profound stillness and calm clarity. From sound rooted in the soundless it may be possible to connect to impermanence rooted in the changeless and time rooted in the timeless.

3.

Concentration

THE ABILITY TO CONCENTRATE IS at the heart of both musical and meditation practice. When we are seriously practicing, performing, or creating music, we are totally focused on the music we are making. It takes a great deal of concentrated energy to put all the necessary elements of harmony, rhythm, melody, and sonic textures together in order to perform or complete a song or piece of music.

Playing or singing scales is one of the touchstones of basic musicianship. Performers at all levels, from beginners to virtuosos, are taught to practice scales to hone and maintain their skills. Jazz musicians dedicate countless hours to learning a wide range of scales, tunings, and modes to broaden the palette of musical shades they can paint with when improvising. Practicing scales, which can feel like an uninspiring, unimaginative, and even unmusical undertaking, requires a great deal of concentration to do well and accurately. But most musicians approach scales with focus and purposefulness, because they know that practicing will lead to the production of beautiful music at some point.

Playing scales is similar to the concentration phase of meditation. During concentration, the meditator is focused on an object—usually the breath—the same way the musician is focused on the moving notes of the scale. Concentrating on the breath, on the face of it, is repetitive, unimaginative, and predictable. It is even more difficult than playing scales, because the body will breathe on its own, without any intentional direction, so the mind and senses are not as engaged as when an instrument is played by a musician. Of course, the mind can wander during playing scales or practicing pieces as well, but it is easier to bring the focus back when you need to manipulate your hands or vocal cords to finish a scale. You can see how adding a musical touch to concentration practice would help to make the practice a little less colorless and uninspiring—and a bit more unpredictable. That's why many of the concentration techniques discussed here engage a musical element to accompany the focus on the breath during meditation.

As a musician you've already developed some degree of these powers of concentration. Why not transfer the basic skill and habit of concentration that's been cultivated by musical practice to meditation practice? Naturally there are differences between the two concentration experiences, but there are some solid similarities upon which to build a meditation practice. And by adding subtle and noninvasive musical touches to traditional contemplative exercises, the path to mindfulness can be made a little less rocky and a little faster to traverse.

POINTILLIST CONCENTRATION—
BLURRING THE EGO

"Your ego is not your amigo."—**As told by Ricky Bell**

Intense concentration on one object is sometimes referred to as one-pointed concentration. I prefer the term *pointillist concentration*—a term that evokes the artists' technique of using discrete points or dots to portray beautiful and serene scenes in nature. You have to stand back to see the big picture that the tiny points are painting.

The essence of pointillist concentration is found right in the word *concentration* itself: a combination of the Latin *cum* (with, join) and *centrum* (center). So *concentration* literally means "connecting to the center." The words *composition* and *composer* have one of the same derivations (*cum*), and both refer to bringing together or arranging different sections into an integrated whole. Normally the center of our awareness is dominated by neurological systems that underpin our sense of self or ego. Evolutionary psychology identifies this monopolizing of our attention as a function of Darwinian natural selection. The "fight or flight" response causes us to be in a state of constant vigilance, evaluating every situation to put our genes in the best position to survive and multiply. The aim of one-pointed concentration, such as focusing exclusively on the breath, is to break this self-referential hold on the center of our consciousness. The object that becomes the focus of our concentration replaces the egocentric agenda that normally dominates our thought patterns.

The self-preservation instinct at the central control system in our brain is constantly flooding our minds with thoughts and emotions. Its agenda is quite primitive—though it may take sophisticated forms and adopt nuanced strategies. Our ubiquitous digital devices have introduced a new phenomenon of FOMO, "fear of missing out," which distracts and fragments our consciousness even more. Our constant planning for the future, dwelling in the past, checking our social media feeds, and working to find solutions to problems may sometimes be useful for Darwinian ends. This frenetic activity could theoretically improve our odds of finding a proper mate, for example. But all this egocentric activity hacks away at our psychic energy, diverting it all for natural selection's selfish and narrow purposes.

When the ego finally vacates the center of our awareness, we no longer have to focus on the many small points of its attention. Standing back, we clearly see the whole picture. No longer held hostage by the egocentric regions of the brain, we can experience reality for what it is, with fewer filters, distractions, and distortions.

KEY STEPS IN YOUR PRACTICE:
BRINGING IT ALL BACK HOME

"Bringing It All Back Home"—**Bob Dylan**

Two young fish were swimming in the ocean when they spotted an old fish swimming toward them. As the old fish approached, he asked, "How's the water?" They didn't respond. After a while one of the young fish turned to his companion and asked, "What the hell is water?"

We normally swim in a sea of thoughts, ideas, and concepts. We mostly don't even notice this perpetual activity that floods our minds. The waters are often turbulent, stirring and muddying everything up. During meditation we realize how insistent and rapid these thought streams are. Many beginners lose heart when they face this reality. They assume that they will never be able to stem this overwhelming tide that invariably interrupts their attempts at calming the waters.

We normally swim in a sea of thoughts,

ideas, and concepts.

. . .

During meditation we realize how insistent and

rapid these thought streams are.

So they try to resist thought or stop thinking all together—a strategy extremely limited in effectiveness. Because thinking, in and of itself, is not the problem. Having ideas and thoughts is a beautiful thing; it often leads to miraculous inventions and artistic achievements. It's also what our human brains were built to do. Where things go awry is in the nature of the thoughts and our relationship to them. We may think we're having a thought, but instead the thought is having us. We may think a thought is shiny and new, but in reality the thought has likely been looping around in our minds for a long while. With practice we can turn this around, so that we can have a calmer, clearer relationship with our thoughts rather than being captured by them.

We may think we're having a thought,

but instead the thought is having us.

. . .

We can have our thoughts work for us,

rather than us work for them.

During meditation we give ourselves a better alternative than listening to the thought loop machine by directing our attention to a more desirable experience. After all, what is more desirable: listening to a shrill, out-of-tune voice or a sweet, harmonious one? Once we start to enjoy the pleasures of peace and the harmonious inner voice that meditation can awaken, we'd much rather dwell in that experience than go wherever the distracted mind would take us. A clearer and more composed mind can observe how and when thoughts and feelings arise and just let them be without being overtaken. We can have our thoughts work for us, rather than us work for them.

When you recognize that you have been caught up in thought this way, you won't feel frustrated or berate yourself; you'll welcome the return of your mindfulness back to the place where you are. You'll feel comfort and reassurance in bringing your attention and intention back to the present moment. Your capacity for mindfulness will strengthen as you realize *I'm bringing my awareness back to the here and now, back to being with my breath. I'm bringing it all back home.*

Of course, soon enough the whole process will happen again. Repetition is as natural to meditation as it is to music. Another idea will hack into your peaceful, harmonious state of mind with an urgent appeal. Once again your attention will wander away. And again you will catch it and bring it all back home, back to the peaceful place of awareness itself. Losing it, catching it, and bringing it all back home is what mindful meditation is all about. And each time it happens, you will feel joy in returning to rest in the here and the now, your true home.

LESSON FROM A JAZZ MASTER: MILES DAVIS
AND BREATHING IN A SILENT WAY

It was prematurely hot and sticky for a day in May, foreshadowing the sauna that New York can be in the summer. That was why I was surprised to see a man sitting in the back of the expensive restaurant wrapped from chin to toe in a thick fur coat. He was sitting regally as if he were holding court, though he was alone at the table. It only compounded my general sense of disbelief and disorientation upon realizing that this bundled-up man was the person I'd had the startlingly good fortune of being invited to lunch with: one of my icons, the great jazz master Miles Davis. And on par with my first sight of him, he didn't disappoint. One thing he said to me that day set my internal tuning fork vibrating, and it is still vibrating as I write this.

I was just getting to know Tommy LiPuma, the noted record producer and Warner Bros. A&R executive. Tommy had suggested that I give him a call when I got to New York, where he was producing Miles Davis's latest album. I took him up on the offer, and to my astonishment Tommy invited me to lunch with him and Miles. By the 1980s Miles Davis was recognized as an unquestioned genius and major innovator in the music world. Since the 1950s he'd pioneered new genres and fusions in music including "cool jazz," psychedelic jazz, and jazz/rock. Almost every significant jazz musician of the era from John Coltrane and Bill Evans to Herbie Hancock and John McLaughlin earned their stripes playing in Miles's band.

Miles was in an expansive mood, friendly and garrulous. He entertained us with story after story, which he told in his gruff, gravelly voice. (I wondered if playing the trumpet for a long time strips the vocal cords of all its satin.) He was a good raconteur and told stories about different clubs, musicians, and cities. At some point he paused and was quiet for what seemed like a considerable time. Then he said that he learned what he thought was the most valuable lesson about music: the important role that silence plays in making music. Airto Moreira, the Brazilian percussionist/composer, revealed it to him. Of course I was intimately familiar with Miles's seminal album *In a Silent Way*, which had been released decades before. I had never really thought about what the title meant. Listening to it again, with the music's long pauses, sharp punctuations, and languorous phrases, I understood what he meant. The performances are testimony to how a melody can be plucked, fully formed from the soundless void, only to return once again to its source: just as when we count beats in bars of music we always return to the one.

———————

Silence is as integral to life as it is to music. And it takes a particular effort to find it.

———————

Miles's statement stuck in my head like a well-crafted hook. When I returned to a meditation practice, it was my guide to a new connection: Silence is as integral to life as it is to music. And it takes a particular effort to find it.

Horn players turn their breathing into music. Meditators turn their breathing into higher states of wakefulness. Focusing on my breath, I felt like a wind instrument, weaving between music and silence. The stillness that I heard at the end of an exhalation was the echo of Miles's muted horn blowing its soundless melodies.

TECHNIQUE: CONSCIOUS BREATHING IN A SILENT WAY

In this meditation practice, which strengthens peaceful concentration, your attention has two main anchors: the bodily sensations associated with breathing and the sounds and silences generated by your respiratory motions and their pauses.

Ease into a relaxed sitting posture. Keep your back straight. This will give your organs room when you breathe and help keep your attention focused. Either close your eyes or fix your gaze a few feet in front of your feet. Place your hands in a comfortable position or mudra.

As you inhale, your abdomen expands outward and your diaphragm rises; as you exhale, your abdomen contracts and your diaphragm falls.

Listen to the sound of your breathing. If you can, breathe only through your nose. If you can't, breathe in a way that is comfortable for you.

As you breathe you are aware of your body breathing and the sound of your breath.

Your abdomen is moving in and out, your chest slightly rising and falling.

You are breathing with your whole body. You can feel your whole body involved in breathing.

Relax your shoulders, your arms, your hands. With every breath, relax a different part of your body. Notice if there is any tension anywhere and ease it. If your awareness turns toward the way your hands are resting on your lap, just note that: Say "hands" silently to yourself. Any way that you can keep your attention on the physical experience of your body is helpful.

As you sit, notice that the tempo of your breathing slows down. As the breath slows down, the mind slows down. As the mind slows down, the world slows down.

Pause for a few moments at the end of your inhalation. Only pause for as long as it's comfortable. Be aware of the stillness and soundlessness within the pause.

Pause again for a few moments after the end of your exhalation. Listen to the silence.

If your attention turns toward ambient sounds, just gently note them and return to the focus on the breath.

You are listening deeply to the sound of your breath; you are feeling your whole body and mind breathing as one.

While you concentrate on your body breathing and the sound(s) it is making, you remain aware of what is happening at this moment: that you are sitting here now, concentrating on your breathing. You are aware that you are aware.

You may also become aware of sensations from the air going in and out of your nostrils. Any bodily sensation that keeps your attention on breathing is useful. Your attention will return toward the chest and abdomen, your anchors.

If you hear a car, silently say to yourself "car" and gently return your focus back to your breathing.

If you hear bodily sounds or internal sounds, note them. If your stomach rumbles, note with your inner voice "rumbling." Then turn your listening back to the sound of your breath.

As your breathing slows down, try to turn down the volume of your breathing with each new breath.

With each new breath, try to keep the sound as inaudible as possible, so that you can barely hear it.

Whatever thoughts arise, when they have run their course, don't analyze them or mull them over. Just draw your focus back to your two anchors: the sounds and sensations of your body breathing. And your awareness that this is happening now.

Keep listening carefully and deeply to the quiet and still moments when you pause between respiratory movements.

If your concentration breaks into a deeper awareness of reality, let it be.

Let it be.

4.

Harmony

IMAGINE A GUITARIST PLAYING A favorite song in her room. As she strums the strings her awareness is centered on the part she is playing. She is totally immersed in the music and is fully present in the moment. Her attention is not scattered; her mind doesn't wander. Her fingers move naturally across the frets to form the chords, and all her bodily movements are in rhythm with the music. Her whole being is unified in the effort of playing that song and feeling the emotion behind it.

———

Meditation elevates this musical
experience of complete inner harmony
and embodied cognition to a higher level
of composure and expanded awareness.

———

Musical performance is only possible when there is such a unification of mind, body, and feeling. If the different parts aren't in harmony, the performance will not work. Meditation also works to harmonize the mind, body, and emotions. To a musician the composed state of meditation is not a strange experience. She already understands how to focus and balance her conscious attention and her bodily movements. In the flow of a musical performance her body and mind seem to have equal knowledge of what notes to play and in what rhythm. The great jazz musician and professor Vijay Iyer has been a pioneer in the study of this phenomenon of "embodied cognition," which recognizes the unification of mental and physical consciousness in musical performance. Meditation elevates this musical experience of complete inner harmony and embodied cognition to a higher level of composure and expanded awareness.

When playing music, it's best to let everything flow naturally without thinking too much. Musicians know that if they have to think about what they're playing, it's not going to come out as they want it to sound: effortless and deeply felt. This is how players "get into a groove"—commonly described as a flow state. The music plays itself, without the interference of overthinking. This strategy of not letting thought interfere with the natural flow of mental and physical movement is common to other skilled activities as well. In athletics it's known as being "in the zone." In samurai culture the ability to focus one-pointedly on the eyes of your opponent to catch the moment when he thinks, and use that minimal opening to attack, is the essential Zen skill of "no-mind"—and the key to a samurai's success in swordplay.

In meditation as in performance, there is a harmonization of the different kinds of cognition—analytical, discursive, judgmental, and so on—with the intuitive and creative aspects of the mind. The mind is composed and balanced, and consciousness is undistracted by thoughts. This eventually comes to include the body, mind, and feelings in a state of harmony. Even though it may seem that the mental aspect dominates during meditation, in most meditative traditions consciousness is experienced through the body as well as the mind. Your whole being is experienced as an organ of awareness. Playing music keeps the mind occupied in a sound, vibration, and feeling, while meditation crosses the border to play in the boundless field of consciousness.

―――――

Your whole being is experienced as an
organ of awareness.

―――――

KEYS STEPS IN YOUR PRACTICE:
THIS IS YOUR TIME

It's helpful to think of the time that you carve out for your practice as your special time to quiet and calm the mind. Your day is filled with urgent tasks, chaotic events, and pressing dilemmas pulling on your attention. Treat this moment as your little window to explore and enjoy clarity of mind and the pleasures of peace.

When your attention wanders during practice, remind yourself that whatever you are thinking about is something you can revisit soon, when your session is done. No matter how important the issue that is occupying your attention may seem, ask yourself whether it can't be put on hold for a little while longer. Is it really worth pulling you away from your special time that you're devoting to developing concentration and pure, relaxed awareness? This is the phase of your life that has a little different rhythm. Now is your time to be clearly aware of *this* very moment in *this* very place.

It's helpful to treat your practice time as sacred time. During this brief break from the ordinary demands on your attention you can work on cultivating your concentration, attention, and wisdom to the exclusion of all else. If your attention is drawn away from the present moment by a pressing issue you are free to acknowledge that issue. You can be aware of it, but then you can let it go. You can nod to it with the realization that it may still be there later, but for right now there's a more important path to follow.

It's helpful to treat your

practice time as sacred time.

You can approach your mindfulness session as a refreshing oasis of tranquility. You can look forward to harmonizing and quieting the mind. You can look forward to a different quality of feeling, a different timbre in your consciousness. Your hefty to-do list will still be there to manage a bit later. Right now, it's your time.

THE BEAUTY OF DISSONANCE

As desirable as finding harmony is, sometimes dissonance can be useful. It can also be very beautiful. We need to make room for disharmony to coexist with harmony. Composers over the centuries have expressed this in their art, embracing dissonance to create moments of profound engagement.

———

When we are visited by dissonance
during meditation in the form of unpleasant
thoughts or emotions, our intention
is to acknowledge them, give them
expression, and allow them their space.

———

Dissonance is also necessary in life. Sometimes it's necessary to raise a jarring voice to pierce mute indifference or complacent acceptance in the face of inequality, unfairness, and social injustice. It's true that contemplative practice encourages equanimity, harmony, and peace. But that doesn't mean that we turn our backs to situations that are not tranquil or harmonious. When we are visited by dissonance during meditation in the form of unpleasant thoughts or emotions, our intention is to acknowledge them, give them expression, and allow them their space. In the same way, we can face unjust situations that need remedying with calmness and compassion.

There is no shortage of dissonance in our culture and society. There is a shortage, however, of harmonic convergence. Contemplatives suggest that we can use more ease to balance the unease. They propose that both individually and as a civilization it's vital that we forge a middle way between harmony and disharmony.

TECHNIQUES

Room Tone

My earliest job after college was at a music editing and sound engineering company in New York. The company edited and mixed music and sound for TV commercials and industrial films. Sound was edited on a clunky device called a Moviola: The film was run through a viewer, and the editor could mark the film by tapping in time to the beat with a chalk pencil.

The film had multiple channels or tracks for sound: There were tracks for dialogue or narration, music, and sound effects. But there was always one track for "room tone," and one of our jobs was to provide that room tone for the project. My supervisor explained that every room has its own tone that you can hear both during dialogue and in the pauses in between; sound editors insisted on having a track dedicated to room tone when it was discovered that lack of room tone was making soundtracks sound artificial and cheap.

When we are sitting in a room, we are seldom aware that in addition to whatever deliberate sounds are being made by men or machines, the room itself is producing its own unique room tone. To begin with, the air within the room is always vibrating and so the room itself vibrates. In addition, there likely are objects in the room propagating sound waves. Besides the sounds that you yourself are creating—sounds that interact with other vibrations—there is probably some kind of machinery generating tones. It could be a computer, modem, clock, lamp, DVR, idling cable box, fan, anything.

Musicians can listen carefully to and distinguish between multiple sounds at the same instant yet still hear them as one. For example, the guitar player in a band has to listen to the rhythm section, the vocalist, and his own playing simultaneously—as the individual parts and as an integrated whole. You can mirror this nondualistic kind of hearing in meditation. While sitting, listen to both the room tone and the sound of your own breathing. If there are outside noises, you can acknowledge them. Nevertheless, try to focus your attention indoors. Tune in to whatever sounds are combining in the room and with your own breathing.

Does it have a tone, or is it toneless? Do you feel like harmonizing the tone of your breathing with the room tone? Is your breathing finding its own way to harmonize with the room tone that is not strictly harmonic?

Musicians can listen carefully to and distinguish between multiple sounds at the same instant yet still hear them as one.

Explore these possibilities. Let whatever happens happen. If you feel like directing your breathing to harmonize with the room tones, do that. If you feel like perceiving the tone of the room as harmonizing with your breathing, do that—or don't do anything at all besides breathing and listening. Just let whatever comes into your experience happen as you sit. Your desire to harmonize or to perceive the tones a certain way may vary during the sitting. Your actual perception of sound and harmony may vary. The fun is to focus your attention on listening and breathing—and to experience your mind composing itself and the moment composing you.

Time Stretching

Here is an exercise to combine counting the breath and harmonizing with the room. When concentrating on the breath, its pace will naturally slow down; deepening the inhalations and exhalations has a well-documented calming effect. But sounding a number in the mind to count the breaths may not keep time with this slower tempo. Stretching the sound of the number so that it lasts as long as the breath makes for a smoother and more harmonious sitting.

While inhaling, slowly stretch out the word *one* so that it lasts as long as the inhalation and listen to the breath and word. While exhaling, do the same stretch, so that the sounded number *one* lasts as long as the exhalation. Concentrate on the sound of the breath and the inner sound of the stretched-out words.

Alternatively, you can stretch the words *in* and *out*. When you say the number in your head, say, "one, in," on the in-breath and "one, out," on the out-breath. Stretch out the words so they last as long as the inhalation or exhalation. Count your breaths from one to ten and then count backward, ten to one.

You can work with both methods at once or alternate them. Either way, remember to pause and to listen to the silence between the breaths. If at any time you feel short of breath, just go back to breathing at a normal pace. It's natural for you to want to pause the time stretch to "catch your breath." Once you feel comfortable in resuming, you can go back to the time stretch.

5.

Practice for the Sake of Practice

MEDITATION IS A PRACTICE THAT shares many common traits with musical practice. When you learn any musical instrument, the first real step is to understand the need to practice. You have to carve out at least thirty minutes every day to sit and practice your instrument. This is essential to making any progress. The same need to commit to consistent practice time holds true for meditation practice.

Practice of any art or sport implies accepting some of the drudgery of repetition. In music it may mean repeating over and over and over the same scales and/or pieces of music. It also means many repetitions of the same movements—of the same integrated body/mind activity. It means concentrating on the practice you are engaged in, even if it is "just" scales. But as Prince sang, you can find great "joy in repetition." Through experience you understand that by repeating the same motions you begin to gain a fluency, a naturalness with the music you are practicing. You can perform complex pieces without thought and with heartfelt spontaneity. In fact, trying to think about what you are doing will only hinder your performance. The music eventually flows through you; you are the performance. And the more and the longer you practice, the more your musicianship benefits.

Meditation is also a practice. It requires the ability to sit a certain number of minutes, every day. Systematic methods such as following or counting the breath are similar to playing scales or études. It is an exercise that feels more natural and easy over time. It is practice that brings you nearer to the heart of meditation or music, practice that tears down the walls between you and the music, or you and peace of mind.

In meditation your mental, emotional, and physical awareness are the instrument you practice on. When you hit obstacles on your meditative path, you realize that with more practice these will be overcome. It's just a matter of having patience and compassion with yourself to continue to sit, to keep practicing. The more and the longer you practice, the more and greater the variety of benefits you will receive.

In meditation your mental,

emotional, and physical awareness

are the instrument you practice on.

John Coltrane, one of the greatest musicians and jazz masters in history, practiced his instrument almost every waking moment, even at the height of his popularity, at least eight hours a day. It is said that even after the Buddha became enlightened, he still sat in meditation for hours every day. Eventually practice in itself becomes the greatest joy.

KEY STEPS IN YOUR PRACTICE:
WHEN YOU SIT, JUST SIT

I once had to fill out a questionnaire in order to attend a meditation retreat. One of the questions asked, "What do you see as the point of your practice at this time?" I answered that there is no point. I was just looking forward to the experience of practice, come what may. I hoped that was the right answer. It was for me.

There is a famous Zen koan, or riddle, that illustrates practicing just to practice. A monk who has studied at a monastery is frustrated with his lack of progress. He finally asks his master to give him one last word of advice. The master says, "When you eat, just eat; when you sit, just sit; when you walk, just walk." The monk protests that he already eats, sits, and walks. The master explains that when the monk eats, his mind is really elsewhere; he is not fully aware and present for the act of eating. If he were truly there while eating he would be absorbed every second in the wondrous reality of the food and his body's miraculous ability to break it down and make use of it.

There's a lighthearted twist on this tale as related in *Zen Is Right Here*, a book of teachings by the founder of the San Francisco Zen Center, Shunryu Suzuki. The student sees his master reading a newspaper while eating breakfast. Recalling the famous Zen dictum "When you eat, just eat," the student points out that his master is not "just eating." Suzuki responds, "When you eat and read the newspaper, just eat and read the newspaper."

At times when we practice an instrument (including our voice instrument) we are practicing with a particular goal in mind. Maybe we have a performance or recording session coming up. So we practice a specific piece or pieces in preparation. Or maybe we are practicing to polish a specific technique that we can use across our repertoire.

When we make music, we just make
music; when we sit, we just sit;
when we practice, we just practice.

But as we can practice for the joy of stillness very often we practice music for the sheer joy of making music. When we close the door of the practice room and pick up our instrument we do it with a certain eagerness. We practice just to practice. We can enjoy our own mastery of a tune; we can be our own appreciative audience. We may have no particular goal other than that the music feels and sounds good to us when we play it.

We can approach our meditation practice the same way. We know that our meditation sessions have the same potential to bring us many valuable experiences. And we can plan them with the same methodical consistency we plan musical practice. When we sit in meditation, we can meditate just to meditate with no particular goal or purpose. When we make music, we just make music; when we sit, we just sit; when we practice, we just practice.

The Count: Four-Bar Breath

Albert Einstein, grand unifier of space and time, was a dedicated amateur violinist. He rarely lacked for skilled accompanists, since his fame attracted the most distinguished musicians of the day to play with him. Apparently his enthusiasm was not evenly matched by talent, and when the legendary concert pianist Vladimir Horowitz took up an offer to accompany him, it is said that Horowitz was so frustrated with Einstein's inability to keep up with the tempo that one day he blurted out with great irony, "Albert, have you no sense of time?"

Counting beats internally is fundamental to music. Counting breaths internally is a fundamental meditation technique. Some traditions start with it; others start and end with it.

One method is to count a four-bar sequence in 4/4 time. The inhalation would be one bar of a four-beat count, the holding of the breath one bar, the exhalation one bar, and finally one bar of pause after the exhalation. The counting of beats and bars is continuous, as if playing a piece of music. The count goes like this:

Inhale	Hold	Exhale	Hold
1234	1234	1234	1234
2234	2234	2234	2234
3234	3234	3234	3234

You can count any number of bars, or rounds of four-beats, that you feel comfortable with: Ten, twelve, or twenty-one bars are a good amount to count. If you count ten four-bar cycles, for example, once you reach the end you can return to one. As with all counting methods, if at any point you lose count, just return to one.

Remember that there is no strict metronome, only a soft internal pulse. No need to keep absolute time dictated by beats per minute (BPMs). Instead we use elastic Einsteinian time that expands and contracts like your breathing apparatus. Your meditative clock is akin to Salvador Dali's famous soft, melting clocks that he created for the surrealistic classic *The Persistence of Memory*. Time is fluid, and tempos can slow down or speed up.

As we've seen, the tempo will naturally slow down the longer you count. It can slow at any point: the beginning, middle, or end of a single bar. After a while you may feel the need to speed up the tempo, as it becomes too difficult to maintain a slower pace. It is all fine. I encourage you to improvise, be flexible and creative. Whatever rhythm your body/mind is requiring at that moment is perfect. Just breathe gently, calmly, and with full attention—and try to keep count.

In the course of meditation you may find the tempo so slow that it is difficult to maintain a four-bar sequence. It may feel natural at that point to just breathe a simple two-bar sequence in 4/4 time. One bar for inhalation, one for exhalation, with no rest in between. This will also give you a chance to get a second wind. Then you can resume your previous four-bar breathing.

Variations on the Counting

There are several variations for the four-bar breath-counting method.

1. Count with a little melody. Lacing a melody with the numbers helps anchor the attention on the breath. Instead of silently speaking the numbers recitative style, you can sing them gently with your inner voice. In other words, you would silently sing "1 2 3 4" with your inner voice instead of just silently speaking it.

I find myself using a little tune most of the time, one that is completely improvised according to the circumstances of the moment. It's not a separate object of attention; the melody is intrinsic to the numbers like any melody and lyric. Except the lyric in this case is uniformly meaningless. Sometimes those are the best kind.

2. Change your time signature: My friend Dr. Sanford Pepper, a noted psychiatrist and gifted jazz pianist, alternates between a bar of 4/4 time (four beats per measure) and a bar of 2/4 time (two beats per measure):

Inhale	Hold	Exhale	Hold
1234	12	1234	12

Sometimes he inserts a 6/4 bar (six beats per measure), during which he extends the exhalation:

Inhale	Hold	Exhale	Hold
1234	12	123456	12

He's found that these variations work best for him in his daily practice.

6.
The Art of Deep Listening

"If the doors of perception were cleansed,
everything would appear to man as it is: infinite."
—William Blake

MUSICALLY MINDED PEOPLE ARE NATURALLY deep listeners. The variety of nuances and qualities that they can discern within a few bars of music is absolutely stunning. They can identify sonic elements such as timbre, amplitude, frequencies, compression, texture, tone, attack, sustain, decay, and release; and there are musical elements such as tempo, harmony, melody, rhythm, and a multiplicity of subdivisions within each of these categories. At the same time a huge spectrum of human emotions can be felt through listening: aggression, tension, melancholy, anticipation, tranquility, levity, transcendence, joy, sensuality, and playfulness—all through changes in volume, tempo, or musical key.

One of the central techniques in meditation is to use the breath as an object of concentration. But maintaining focus on the breath is not easy. Deep listening can help make your breath capture your attention the same way an alluring melody can. Listen to the sound of your breathing as if you're listening to the sound of music. Listen to your inhales and exhales with the same degree of intense interest and subtle discernment. Many of the same characteristics that you listen for in music may appear during your concentration on the breath. The sound of your own breathing is beautiful; it is the sound of your life.

Deep listening can help make your breath
capture your attention the same way an
alluring melody can.

Another method of concentration is to be aware of environmental sounds. This method is usually adopted after the mind has been stabilized by focusing on the breath. During sitting you may become aware of various sounds that pop up around you: the sounds of traffic, birds, voices, hammers, and so on. Noting these sounds as appearing in the field of your consciousness without getting caught by them, and knowing that you are aware of them, is a way to cultivate mindfulness. Again the ability to deeply listen as developed through music is being used as a tool of meditation.

There are modes of meditation that combine both these techniques of following the breath and noting environmental sounds. It is sometimes called "dual awareness" and is also an effective practice for developing both concentration and insight.

During meditation it is normal to be distracted by thoughts. You hear the sound of hammering outside your window, and you wonder what the construction is about, when it will stop—before you know it you've spun out of your seat and into a story. These thoughts are often spoken by our inner voice—mulling over talking points for an upcoming interview, or replaying the argument you had with your spouse, or pondering doubts about the tone you used to answer an email. While listening to music in a serious manner we've learned to quiet this inner voice, or at least put it on "pause" so that we can focus on the sound of music. When we do get distracted by thoughts, the sound of our breathing will interrupt and bring us back to the breath. This becomes a reflexive process when we have made deep listening a way of attending to the breath.

---

*If you can listen deeply, you not only listen to music with a refined cognitive awareness, but you **feel** the music with your body and soul.*

The ability to quiet the inner voice and engage in deep listening is also an essential quality of daily mindfulness. We can really tune in to what another person is saying and hear them clearly. Dialing down the noise of our chattering inner voice and using our ability of subtle discernment—of keen observation—we can receive the various nuances in what the other person is trying to communicate. Most musicians are not aware that they have the capability to apply deep listening to other areas in the course of their daily lives. When they do apply deep listening, it can yield great benefits to their interpersonal relationships, communication skills, and emotional intelligence.

Deep listeners hear in multiple ways. If you can listen deeply, you not only listen to music with a refined cognitive awareness, but you *feel* the music with your body and soul. It is a holistic experience that can engage your whole being. A discerning audience can tease apart a stunning variety of sonic, emotional, and musical elements on a granular level.

This capacity for multidimensional awareness involving mind and body can be used to great effect during meditation. One of the most common methods of meditation—concentration on the breath—can be enlivened by focusing on both the sounds and the bodily sensations involved in breathing. In this mode, as you breathe your upper body rises with the inhalation and falls with the exhalation; your abdomen expands with the inhalation and contracts with the exhalation. You can focus on either the torso rising and falling or the abdomen expanding and contracting. Some followers of Zen emphasize focusing on the abdomen during meditation, paying special attention to actively contracting the abdomen as the maximum amount of oxygen is expelled. Others focus on the rising and falling of the chest, and still others include both bodily movements. You can choose whichever method you prefer. What's important is to attentively follow the breath both by listening and by maintaining awareness of the movement of the body. Once we achieve this, we can also listen to the silence between breaths. It is in that pause that we often find our greatest peace and gain our deepest insights.

NO FILTER

When a comment is made that someone "has no filter," it's generally interpreted as a critical observation of a lack of social etiquette. In the context of pure awareness, however, having no filter is quite the opposite; it's something we aspire to. Just as an envelope filter in audio production will squeeze and distort waveforms, our mental filters work the same way in manipulating the truth. In mindfulness we have the capacity to dissolve our filters and let the pure signal through—gradually erasing the concepts, beliefs, cultural biases, and personal preferences that otherwise filter our daily lives. We open ourselves up to whatever arises; we are completely receptive: like an antenna attuned to all possible frequencies.

We presume nothing; we prejudge nothing
and are certain of nothing.

We try to carry this unfiltered understanding to everything that confronts us in daily life. We presume nothing; we prejudge nothing and are certain of nothing. This way we can truly listen and hear what is being said—and at the same time what is not being said. We can come closer to a clearer view and a deeper understanding.

TRANSITIONING FROM CONCENTRATION
TO MINDFULNESS

Using a technique that focuses on the breath as the main anchor of meditative attention is a time-tested way of developing composure, harmony, and strong powers of concentration. After you've practiced focusing on the breath to the point that you can remain relatively unified, composed, and undistracted, you may feel the inclination to transition into a state of open and receptive awareness. Some characterize this as transitioning from concentration to mindfulness. Progressing from focusing awareness on the breath to focusing on the energy of awareness itself can occur organically. In fact, that kind of organic, gradual progression from concentration to insight and realization has been the basic method of many schools of Zen through the ages.

Yet concentration and mindfulness are not states of consciousness that radically diverge. There isn't a well-defined border between them; they are permeable and can blend into each other. Building the skill to keep the mind composed and stable in concentration can lead to the ability to improve clarity, equanimity, and harmony for being attentive to the whole of your experience. Once you have liberated your consciousness from the restrictive domination of your egocentric agenda through meditative concentration, you are free to expand your wisdom and compassion in infinite ways. Mindfulness can be a spontaneous and natural evolution from concentration.

It's understandable that we would want to shift from restricted concentration—holding our attention in one place—into a free zone, where we can be open and attentive to whatever arises. But unless the powers of concentration are developed enough to support the freedom of receptive awareness, wandering into the free zone can lead to mindless roaming. It's best to have already built a pretty solid foundation in a regular concentration practice before attempting to meditate in open awareness.

FROM DEEP LISTENING IN THE STUDIO
TO RUTHLESS ATTUNEMENT

Imagine what happens when you carry over the habit of deep listening from music into life. It can make the difference between a deal and no deal. Because when you really listen to someone and calibrate your sensitivity to what they *mean*—which is as much in their tone, tempo, and timbre as in the words they say (and don't say)—you can get a good understanding of what they really want. And that insight into their thinking can open up the common ground between you. It can help persuade a television producer to give your underscore a chance or untangle a difficult contretemps with a significant other.

This kind of deep listening draws upon other features in the mindfulness ecosystem: patience, calmness, empathy, and perseverance. I've learned the art of deep listening from watching successful studio engineers deploy their listening skills to delicately balance the egos of their artist, producer, and record company clients while bringing out the best in a song. Studio magicians such as the go-to mixer Dave "Hard Drive" Pensado, from whom I'm always learning, uses his attentive talents to calmly and patiently interpret the oblique and at times divergent desires of his clients. And though he may have a better sense of where to take a track than a client does in a moment of inspiration, he'll hang back until he absolutely needs to weigh in with a mixing move that can save the record. He would say,

"Everyone's a singer when they talk. It doesn't always matter who's listening; people just want to be *heard*."

Sometimes, if you're patient and empathetic enough to really listen, you can dig up common ground in the most unlikely places.

———

"It doesn't always matter who's listening;

people just want to be heard."

———

A turning point for me came in an encounter with Eric Wright—known as "Eazy-E"—the former drug dealer, pioneering leader of the gangsta rap firebrands N.W.A., and founder of controversial Ruthless Records. N.W.A. had recently become a global phenomenon when their supertalented producer Dr. Dre split from the group. Eazy-E, along with Ruthless's cofounder and band manager, Jerry Heller, needed to find producers to fill the vacuum and work on his second solo album. Shortly thereafter my partner, Bret "Epic" Mazur, and I started to get calls from Jerry Heller. Apparently, they had been following our careers as a production team in the early '90s. Problem was, as much as I admired Dre's production and the group's authentic portrayals of the hard life of inner-city youth, I had serious objections to some of their lyrics. I was opposed to their casual misogyny, homophobia, and glorification of violence. Of course, that was a feature of their enormously popular outlaw personae and an outgrowth of their particular experiences, but I couldn't see being a part of it. So I would ask Bret to tell him that we were not interested, now or ever.

But Jerry was persistent and didn't take no for an answer. Finally, Bret convinced me that we should at least *hear them out*. As we walked into the meeting at the Ruthless Records offices in Woodland Hills, my guard was up. But within minutes we were disarmed by how laid back, frank, respectful, and unassuming they both were. And the mood was further lightened by the warm glow of the father-son-type bond between Eazy-E and Jerry that suffused the room.

In person Eazy-E had an undeniable charm. He never showed any of the callousness, cruelty, or women- and gay-bashing aggression that was part of his image. He proposed that we produce half of his next solo album, a surefire hit. But when I insisted that he guarantee that the music we provided would not be a soundtrack for slurs against gays or women or the glorification of violence, he laughed.

A few days after the meeting Eazy-E called, saying he wanted to drop by my studio. He hung out as Bret and I worked on a hip-hop remix for Prince. Leaning way back in his chair, his pockets overflowing with cash and bags of weed, he was the same quietly confident presence. We all vibed to the music, sharing the same love for the funky, streetwise, innovative, devastatingly raw beauty of hip-hop. In the months that followed we would continue to get together to listen and to talk, and I found myself growing to like this obviously gifted man I had once refused to sit down with.

We never came to an agreement with Eazy-E about our conditions for working on his album. But we did bring our group Blood of Abraham, whose lyrics were focused on spirituality and social justice, to Eric and Jerry.* They were signed to Ruthless, Eazy-E executive produced and performed on the record, and the band was in the middle of promoting it when Eazy-E tragically succumbed to AIDS in 1995.

---

* Jerry referred to this in his book, *Ruthless* (New York: Simon Spotlight Entertainment, 2006), 285–86.

KEY STEPS IN YOUR PRACTICE: VISUALIZATION

Visualization can be an aid to cultivating concentration. While some prefer maintaining a steady and soft focus on the ground or on an object in front of them, others may find that having a mental image or images to help anchor the attention can be useful. If it helps you to visualize counting your breaths as you begin to develop your concentrative powers, even if it's only for a brief period, then go for it. Keep in mind that visualization is used to complement your musical skill set of deep listening and bodily cognition.

As you connect a mental image to your breathing, it's best to keep the visualization simple. That way you are less likely to get caught up in what you're "seeing" and lose your rhythm. Once your attention has stabilized, you can experiment with stopping the visualization (just as you would stop counting if you were using one of the counting methods). While staying conscious of the breath, open up your awareness to your whole experience, both internally and externally. The stream of thoughts and feelings may continue to flow, but instead of clinging to them you will just watch them like a fan watching a ball game from a seat in the stadium on a pretty summer evening.

Visualization may be useful when
you find it particularly challenging to
maintain your attention on the breath.

Here are some ways to visualize while using the most basic method of simply counting the breaths:

1. Visualize the numbers as you count your breaths. For example, as you count one, visualize the number 1 going up a hill on the inhalation and then going down the hill on the exhalation. Continue following the breath while visualizing the number you are counting as it goes up and down the hill.

2. Visualize the number approaching from a distance on the inhalation and fading toward the distance on the exhalation.

3. Sports fans can visualize the timer at a basketball game as the red digital numbers keep count of the breaths.

4. Visualize pebbles dropping into a beautiful, blue placid lake. As the pebbles drop, concentric waves are formed on the surface.

5. As you inhale, visualize a pebble rolling off a cliff or ledge and dropping into the water. As you exhale, visualize the waves radiating on the surface as the pebble sinks below. Repeat to yourself silently with each breath: "One pebble dropping into the water, one pebble sinking beneath the waves."

I know a passionate dog owner who visualizes walking her dog as she breathes: "On the inhalation, count *one*, taking the dog outside; on the exhalation, count *one*, walking the dog back home; inhalation, *two*, taking the dog outside; exhalation, *two*, bringing the dog back home," and so on. To me this sounds a bit complicated, but she insists that it works for her.

You can experiment with different mental images that sync to the rhythm of your breathing. Visualization may be useful when you find it particularly challenging to maintain your attention on the breath. But once you reach a state of relative calm and clarity, it's sometimes useful to let go of the images and allow for the transparency of the present moment. Keeping your mind clear and free of images while moving from one-pointed concentration toward the receptivity of mindfulness allows for greater openness to whatever arises in your field of experience.

TECHNIQUES

Seeing Sounds

During this meditation practice, your breath is the anchor, the steady rhythm section, the mental metronome. While still listening to the sound of your breath, open up your awareness to hear other sounds that occupy the landscape around you. Traffic, voices, machinery, airplanes, birds—all manner of sounds may arise in your awareness. Treat them as images that dot the landscape and try not to label them as either pleasant or unpleasant. They are a fact—they are just there.

The sounds occur in the field of awareness; you visualize them in their place in the sphere of consciousness. They may rise and fall, appear and disappear. A particularly loud sound may come in and overshadow others, like the sound of a plane that blankets the songs of birds. As you listen to the sounds outside your body, you still hear the sound of your breathing in relation to the other sounds. It's comparable to the steady basso ostinato, or looping bass line pattern, in a Bach passacaglia or the guitar riff in a Jimi Hendrix rocker. The outside sounds are the "top line," or improvised melodies that play above the rhythm of the breath. The sounds inside and outside become integrated; they are all members of one ensemble.

If you are sitting indoors, it is easier to hear the sound of your own breathing. Sitting outdoors, you may have to breathe more energetically in order to make the breath audible. As you become aware of a new sound, just note that you are hearing this new sound. When you note the arising, sustaining, and decaying of sounds, you are fully in the present moment; you are totally attuned to what is happening now. Noting this in a calm, relaxed, but very aware state brings clarity and stability to the mind. As different sounds arise around you, you may develop the impression of being in the midst of a vast empty field of awareness with pockets of sound objects all around. The randomness and spontaneity of sounds is like the paint splatters on canvas. It's as if you are seeing sound.

The sounds inside and outside become integrated; they are all members of one ensemble.

In the practice of "seeing sounds," you experience yourself in a spacious and open field of consciousness. This field has no boundaries but does have limitations, unseen and unknown. The sounds themselves are neither pleasant nor unpleasant, but the experience *of hearing* them and being conscious that they are in your field is very pleasant. You can locate the different sounds in different areas to the west or east, above or below—in all different directions. It's as if you are seeing them across an expansive 360-degree panorama. Here are the birds, there is the traffic; here is the ringing in my ears, there is the breath. There and here are inseparable—here is there and there is here—because you and the landscape are now one field of consciousness.

I once attended a silent vipassana meditation class in the courtyard of a high school. It was after the school day had ended, so there were very few people left on campus. But we were sitting outdoors and there still were plenty of ambient sounds—birds, traffic, planes. Some of the meditation students remarked to the teacher that they had trouble concentrating because all the noises were so distracting. The teacher encouraged the students to ignore the sounds and to try to focus on the breath.

If the students had integrated the sounds into their mindfulness practice, they might have had a more satisfying experience. They might have taken pleasure in the act of listening, in the experience of how the present moment expresses itself in sound and in the pure joy of being aware of sound and its constant companion, silence.

Fortissimo-Pianissimo-Fortissimo

This method plays with the dynamic range in the auditory volume of your breathing. Your ability to focus on sound and to listen deeply plays a big part in this practice. Although the method is called "fortissimo-pianissimo-fortissimo," the dynamic instructions are not to be taken literally; instead of "extremely loud–extremely soft–extremely loud," think of these dynamics as "pretty audible–barely audible–pretty audible."

Start breathing in a comfortably audible range. Your focus will be on the expansion and contraction of your belly and the sound of your breath. This breathing is labeled "fortissimo," because it is loud enough to wake you up when your mind drifts off. It doesn't have to be at ear-splitting volume, or anywhere near it. As long as you can easily hear your breath the volume level qualifies as fortissimo. Count twelve breaths at this very audible level.

The next set will be very soft. You want to get as quiet as you can while you can still barely hear your breathing. This method takes a great deal of concentration because you should really have to listen to yourself very carefully in order to hear it. During this stage I sometimes picture an exacting conductor hushing a small ensemble at a particularly delicate passage while they play behind a soloist. Count twelve breaths at pianissimo.

Alternate between the two volumes. As with all breathing methods, the pauses between breaths are very important. After the inhalation hold your breath for a time that feels comfortable. Rest in the stillness and listen deeply. After expelling the air from your lungs during the exhalation, hold the contraction of your abdomen and lungs. Sit still in full awareness and continue to listen deeply.

During this meditation you will be expending substantial energy on the different amplitude modulations, so depending on your lung power these pauses may be relatively short. However, moving between the two volumes allows for continued concentration without exhaustion.

7.

Patience and Perseverance

ONE DAY PABLO CASALS, THE world-renowned cellist, was interrupted while practicing his instrument by a student who arrived early for a lesson. Casals was ninety-three at the time. The student was surprised that his teacher, the most celebrated and esteemed cellist of the day, had been concentrating so much on practicing that he hardly noticed the student's presence. When he asked Mr. Casals why, at age ninety-three and at the top of the musical world, he still needed to practice, the cellist answered, "Because it feels like I'm making progress."

Playing a passage of music takes patience. It takes facing failure. It takes a degree of self-compassion and understanding, not getting too frustrated with yourself when you just can't get it. It takes the will to try again after a flubbed performance, the will to slowly practice a difficult passage until it is finally mastered. All musicians who want to perform, no matter how talented, must have the necessary patience to overcome their own perceived mediocrity, the patience to overcome the disappointment in not meeting self-imposed standards of perfection, the patience to practice that sequence ad infinitum until the song is just right.

Meditation also requires patience. It requires not getting frustrated when we lose focus. It accepts the restless and chaotic nature of the mind, and it works by gently guiding our attention back to the object of concentration. It recognizes that we may become forgetful and unaware of the present moment for long periods and asks that we calmly refocus without self-recrimination. It requires overcoming disappointment in not reaching nirvana within an arbitrary time limit. It requires the patience to practice day after day, even though it seems we are making little progress.

Patience demonstrated over a long period of time and in the face of many failures becomes perseverance. To participate in a performance in any serious way requires persistent patience. It calls upon the intention to endure suffering and defeat. It calls upon the ability to persevere through humiliation, frustration, and disappointment, all while maintaining a sense of calm, self-compassion, and faith that our trial and error will be ultimately worthwhile. It calls upon a ninety-three-year-old master cellist to steadfastly practice in order to keep making progress.

THE PLEASURES OF PEACE

"Oh the Pleasures of Peace are infinite and they
cannot be counted."
—Kenneth Koch, "The Pleasures of Peace"

In my travels through Thailand, India, Japan, and China I've
noticed that wherever there were figures of the Buddha meditating, he always appeared to be smiling. In Thailand he had
a bigger smile, in Japan more of a half smile, but everywhere I
went there was at least the glimmer of a smile playing on his lips.

In meditation, the mind, heart, and body can reach a place of
pure harmony, stillness, and calm. These are some of the pleasures of peace that we can delight in. Finding peace in concentration can create a sense of joy, a feeling of freedom. We can
identify different pleasure centers in our bodies, but the greatest
source of pleasure can come from just enjoying our total mind-
body awareness.

Quiet bliss, pleasant calm, and meditative joy are some of
the observable fruits of meditation. Some teachers discourage
emphasizing joy and advocate going beyond pleasure and non-
pleasure to achieve a state of complete equanimity. In the cultivation of mindfulness the practice is to attempt to be conscious
of feelings, perceptions, or thoughts without evaluating whether
they are pleasant or unpleasant. Others warn against getting

stuck in feelings of bliss or getting too attached to "meditative joy," because those who do may be distracted from all the other benefits of practice. And it is true that too much emphasis on the joys of concentration can hinder the progress into mindfulness. But for most—especially those of us who do not have speed-dial access to total contemplative absorption and equanimity—if the pleasures of peace arise during meditation they are a treasure to enjoy. After all, once we flow into a state of pure, selfless awareness we recognize that meditative joy is our natural state. The pleasures of peace are not transmitted from the outside like some drug or intoxicant; instead they emerge from deep within us.

Finding peace in concentration can
create a sense of joy, a feeling of freedom.

Joy can be an effective incentive to work through our laziness or resistance to practice. Sometimes when I procrastinate in starting a session it's the prospect of peace and its many pleasures that draw me in.

We often think of silence as an absence of sound, but silence is the presence of nonsound that incubates the potentialities of sound. We think of stillness as an absence of movement, but it is actually the presence of the ground of being. We think of peace as the absence of conflict, but it is the presence of a pure and pleasing calm: a relaxed and liberated awareness.

Pleasure is often thought of as the satisfaction of desire. When an object is desired there is tension and pressure until that desire is satisfied. There is the agitated energy of the struggle to achieve or grasp the object of ambition. Once the desire is satisfied, the feeling of relief and joy emerges. The tension of desire is released, the pressure is discharged, the struggle is resolved—and for the moment there is a great and pleasurable sense of peace and happiness. There is the feeling of letting go: no more need to struggle. In a musical setting desire and its appeasement parallel the classic sequence of crescendo, climax, release, and the final peaceful silence. But the happiness that comes with the satisfaction of desire is transitory. Soon the next desire comes along, and the cycle of crescendo, climax, and release begins again.

Contemplative practice also leads to the relaxing of tension and the release of pressure. It is very much like the process of desire and appeasement. There is the sense of letting go, of letting it be. The grasping fist unclenches, and the hand and heart open up. The struggle is over, and peace prevails. Mindfulness of the pleasures of peace can bring a subtler and more durable kind of freedom and profound joy to the practitioner than the transitory joy of material pleasure. This kind of joy harmonizes mental, emotional, existential, and physical aspects. In its synthesis of these different aspects it generates a peaceful and steadying undertone that can continue throughout daily life.

DYNAMIC BREATHING AND THE
PLEASURES OF PEACE

Becoming aware of the pleasures of peace as they arise during meditation is an effective focus for concentration and mindfulness. Just as we do with the breath, we acknowledge joy as it arises in our field of awareness. Notice how your mind and body—in fact your whole being—experiences peaceful joy.

Soon we can experience quiet joy during all the phases of breathing, at times even when not in meditation.

We can approach our awareness of the four phases of breathing as analogous to the classic cycle of crescendo, climax, release, and peace. When we inhale, we can be mindful that we are taking in particles of energy that will nourish us. As our torso rises and our abdomen expands, we are filling ourselves with nutrients that are energizing and strengthening us. This is the crescendo or building-up phase. Next, at the height of our inhalation we briefly hold on to the breath in the climax phase. Physical and mental movement stops, while we focus on holding this position of expansion. Then we let go; we release what we've been holding in. When we've exhaled as much as we can, our mind and body finally reach a state of stillness, silence, and peace. We pause again before we take the next breath. We enjoy the calm stillness and listen to the silence.

This mode eventually leads to deeper and longer moments of joyful peace that last throughout the breath cycle. Soon we can experience quiet joy during all the phases of breathing, at times even when not in meditation.

The conscious enjoyment of the pleasures of peace that arise during meditation can effectively focus our practice. We look forward to our next sitting when we know it can bring the kind of deep satisfaction that is pleasurable in mind, soul, and body.

KEY STEPS IN YOUR PRACTICE:
NO EXPECTATIONS

When you sit down for a meditation session, approach it with no expectations. Every meditation experience is different from the ones before. We are all different from moment to moment, and so are our experiences. Many times, practitioners have powerful experiences during meditation. They can be particularly joyful, or insightful, or stunningly revealing experiences. It's natural then to anticipate a repetition of one of these experiences. We cling to the memory of that experience, and that attachment colors our current reality. But that very clinging and the emotion of anticipation prevent the spontaneous arising of anything similar to those coveted experiences.

On the one hand, the memories of pleasant or illuminating experiences during meditation are great motivators in support of our practice. They help propel us back to the seat of awakening. However, it's advisable to have an open heart when starting a meditation. Let whatever will happen, happen. Some days the sessions may just leave us with a faint undertone of tranquility. On other days something may stress us out so strongly that we barely can find a few seconds of quiet attention. No two days will ever be experienced exactly the same, so remember: patience.

TECHNIQUE: THE LITTLE REFRAIN

At the beginning of a meditation session you may find it helpful to repeat a very short but calming refrain. Try these four powerful words: *calm, relaxed, peaceful, now.*

As you take an in-breath you quietly think to yourself: *calm.*
Just that one-syllable word: *calm.*
Next, on the out-breath you say: *relaxed.*
On the next in-breath: *peaceful.*
And the next out-breath: *now.*

Besides helping you concentrate on the breath, these particular words have a subtle power to soften your mind and help bring about a state of peace. After relaxing the body by "tuning the drum" (page 41), this refrain is a useful next step in quieting down the restless mind.

You can repeat the refrain as often as it feels natural. Divide the words up any way you like as well. If you are just beginning your session, you may find that your mind is not stable enough to stay focused on the one word for each breath. In that case, simply assign two words each for the in-breath and the out-breath:

In-breath: *calm, relaxed.*
Out-breath: *peaceful, now.*

When you find that you're in a relaxed state, you may slow down the flow and instinctively stretch each word over both an in-breath and an out-breath:

First breath: *calm.*
Second breath: *relaxed.*
Third breath: *peaceful.*
Fourth breath: *now.*

Sometimes I use the in-breath to think the word and the out-breath as a faint echo. So:

In-breath: *calm.*
Out-breath: *calm* (soft echo).
In-breath: *relaxed.*
Out-breath: *relaxed* (soft echo).
In-breath: *peaceful.*
Out-breath: *peaceful* (soft echo).
In-breath: *now.*
Out-breath: *now* (soft echo).

As you proceed, the particular cadence of the refrain can be improvised depending on your particular state of being. It doesn't really matter how you phrase it, but keeping the four-word order and one of these basic templates is most effective. At times you may use the refrain as a way to begin your session and then move on to another technique. It's quite useful as a bridge taking you from restless, mundane preoccupations to greater mental stability. At other times you may enjoy using the refrain as your primary technique throughout the whole session.

If you're doing this practice for any considerable length of time, it's helpful to mindfully insert a pause or silence between breaths. As with most techniques that include focusing on the breath, listening deeply to the silence while you pause between the exhalations and inhalations is important. Listening to the silences in between the words will help deepen your calmness and strengthen your concentration and awareness.

Another neat thing about the refrain is its mobility. You may find the refrain popping up during the course of your everyday activities. It may just suddenly appear while you're in the middle of some ordinary endeavor. Or you may use it during a stressful moment as a way to calm yourself and find some equanimity. For example, an intern for a very successful but verbally abusive composer used it repeatedly to keep his cool on the job. This simple, durable refrain is what record companies would call a "legacy asset."

8.

Mindfulness and Creativity

I'VE KNOWN MANY TALENTED SONGWRITERS and composers who could create inspired and original sketches but could never produce a finished work. They just didn't have the necessary focus to bring their brilliant but undeveloped ideas to fruition. They would get sidetracked or impatient, lose interest, or feel discouraged in some way. Meditation practice refines and strengthens the powers of concentration indispensable to refining an idea or work of art to bring it to completion. Good concentration also implies the qualities of patience and persistence vital to seeing a project through to the end.

Meditation can also make us better listeners and, thereby, better musicians. It's thought that since meditation frees the intuition, and since much of creativity springs from intuition, meditation can unleash creative potential. The acclaimed film auteur David Lynch has written that meditation expands consciousness—and more consciousness equals more creativity. For him meditation is a way to dive into a limitless sea of consciousness, one in which you can catch the "big fish" of great new ideas. When we more specifically refine the art of listening within meditation, we can tap into deeper, more original perceptions to inspire creative generation—musical or otherwise. By quieting the recklessly active judgmental faculties, meditation affords the intuitive sense more breathing space and airtime in the mind. When I first settled into a consistent meditation practice, it released a flood of poems over the course of a few years. I had never stopped composing music or songs, but poetry was a whole new form of expression. I'm not sure exactly why, but it seemed that because I was spending time listening deeply in silence, I was hearing fresh sounds flowing from a different source.

Turning off that inner judging voice is important in another way, which Lynch touched upon when he accurately observed that "negativity is the enemy of creativity." A persistent internal critic who is always highlighting imperfections in our creative ideas can lead to paralysis. The most innovative and ingenious ideas will never see the light of day if a cloud of self-criticism is constantly throwing shade. Mindfulness and meditation train us to observe events, including our own ideas and thoughts, in a noninvasive and nonjudgmental fashion. It allows for a free-flowing stream of creativity, unobstructed by preconceptions, prejudgments, or other mental formations. This laissez-faire approach to the emergence of ideas can channel the flow of raw creative energy into constructive completion.

Peter Scaturro, an accomplished composer, musician, and producer currently working as the senior music producer for Sony PlayStation, once explained to me how meditation can lift a creative block: "I would be in the throes of the creative process when a voice would constantly interrupt. It seemed like it was always hovering over my shoulder. This voice would find fault with whatever I had just composed. And as soon as I made a little progress, the voice would interrupt again. I couldn't ever get anything finished. Once I learned how to meditate, the voice started to fade. I learned how to relax and make necessary adjustments without the soul-killing negativity of that critical voice. Eventually the voice went away."

Jazz composer Thelonious Monk said, "There are no wrong notes, only better choices." Creativity requires making choices, and mindfulness trains us to make such choices: every time we have a feeling or idea and decide to not get caught up in it. It makes sense that training in the observation of ideas and thoughts in a nonattached, noncritical way can help us discern constructive choices during the creative process. And our powers of concentration and physical stamina can help to keep our undistracted attention on shaping the object of creativity.

Refining the art of letting go during meditation may also prove useful when applied to the creative process. In mindfulness practice we learn to disengage from thoughts, feelings, ideas, and concepts. We learn to observe our present reality without identifying with it. Likewise, artists can also act as spectators unattached to the work. Creators sometimes have difficulty letting go of their creations. They are never satisfied and get caught up with endless tweaking and tinkering. They feel they still haven't lived up to the grand idea behind the creation; as an archetype of the artistic master, Leonardo da Vinci, said, "Art is never finished, only abandoned." It's difficult to maintain the balance between the ideal of perfection and the reality, but ultimately all creators need to abandon their creations and give them up to the world. Since in mindfulness, we repeatedly go through the motions of disengaging from our creations, we can become pretty good at rocking that letting-go song.

*The practice of intense concentration
and the energy of pure, relaxed
awareness can help clear the way
for creativity to flow freely.*

Of course the formal practices of meditation and mindfulness are not necessary for creativity. There have been countless influential creators who were anything but exemplars of stable mindfulness or relaxed, nonjudgmental awareness. And there have been innumerable artists and innovators who have demonstrated prodigious powers of concentration and epic flights of transcendence and ingenuity who were total strangers to the formal practices of mindfulness or meditation. But as we've seen, these practices can help creative people stay clear-eyed and focused on realizing their artistic visions. They can help remove blocks when creativity is stymied by false perceptions, fragmented consciousness, or overactive self-criticism and despair. In a time when stress, anxiety, and attention deficits are pervasive and fed by technological overstimulation, these practices can be of great value. The practice of intense concentration and the energy of pure, relaxed awareness can help clear the way for creativity to flow freely. Tempering the distractions and toning down the discouraging and emotionally discordant notes that resound through the culture, these practices can bring a harmonious freedom that can help support a lifetime of unbridled creativity.

FINDING YOUR VOICE:
COLTRANE'S "GIANT STEPS"

Central to being an artist or musician is finding your own unique voice. There are different ways of approaching this vague concept, but it usually begins by finding the inner voice that speaks from deep within the psyche. It is this voice that is always talking to us, and in the case of musical minds, singing to us. When we have thoughts, it is this inner voice that only we hear expressing our thoughts. Both in meditation and artistic creativity we seek to find our voice. Once we find it, though, what happens next is quite different.

John Coltrane is considered one of the giants among the pantheon of jazz masters. His music is revered for many reasons, including its bold originality and earnest spirituality. There is a distinctive and immediately identifiable quality in his voice that evokes profound and powerful feelings.

Coltrane's transformative sound evolved in a very public way. Almost every artist begins the journey by imitating personal icons. It is said that when he was beginning to try out his own voice, he used the saxophone to emulate the sound of his mother calling him home at night when he was a child playing outdoors. He eventually progressed from evoking his mother's voice to expressing countless other worldly and otherworldly voices.

Coltrane was a successful musician when he faced his greatest personal crisis: Addicted to heroin, he was forced from his perch with the popular Miles Davis band. He then had what he called a "spiritual awakening." For the rest of his life he dedicated himself to voicing his deep feelings for what he intuited as the transcendent and divine truth.

Coltrane explored many traditions, with an emphasis on West African and Indian spiritual teachings. He wanted his music and his faith to be one seamless whole, a medium through which he and his audience could unite with the supreme consciousness. When he traveled to East Asia, he made a deep study of Japanese music and culture and, among many innovations, famously brought the Japanese pentatonic scale into the mainstream of jazz composition. His sound grew to evoke heightened states of divine peace and love. The titles of his songs—"A Love Supreme," "Om," "Ascension," "Meditations," "Selflessness"—express in words the sublime feelings that the music transmits. He selflessly gave over his voice to the voice of the universal consciousness that he believed is the one divine source of all being.

In the end, finding your voice is not hard at all; it's like finding your finger or your foot. Because the only voice you ever do find is always your own. All our perceptions of reality— everything we hear, read, see or think about—are interpreted to us by our own inner voice. Too often, however, we don't realize this and just lap up everything our voice tells us as if it's all truth and the only truth. It's as if we are all completely blind, and our inner voice narrates for us what is happening in the outside world.

The only voice you ever do find

is always your own.

The problem is that the reality this voice is framing for us is multidimensional, extremely complicated, and always in flux. We crave an understanding of what is happening in our world, and we have to rely on this voice, which is, after all, always there. But that only gives us reality from one angle out of an infinity of angles. Inevitably the story our voice tells us about what is happening is deeply flawed. As Seneca wrote, "It's not activity that disturbs people, but false conceptions of things that drive them mad." Sometimes, in order to get with what's really going on we need to give over our small personal voice to the impersonal, universal, and timeless voice, as Coltrane did.

We have moments when we intuit that the ultimate source of this voice, this personal ego agenda, is very vast. The source may be hidden from us, but somehow we know it's there. We sometimes feel our hearts beating and know that there is a very powerful, unseen force behind the beating of our heart. We're not the ones beating our hearts.

Selfless Sheets of Sound

Coltrane developed his "sheets of sound" method of playing many notes with almost superhuman speed. This technique requires an ability to hold an exhalation for an extraordinary length of time. Some Zen meditation schools similarly emphasize holding the exhalation for as long as possible during meditation; some even believe that without this breathing technique the student will never achieve *kenshō?* (a Japanese term for enlightenment). Since Coltrane's playing style required extremely long exhalations, it's believed by some that he achieved kenshō? just like a Zen meditator. According to this view his "sheets of sound" style of playing was an original way of meditating.

For a musician like Coltrane, it only takes one long breath to produce a multiplicity of sounds. From the one come the many; from the oneness of the essential consciousness arises the multiplicity of the phenomenal world. Whatever the source of his genius, Coltrane communicates universal truth in an impassioned and singularly personal voice. It eloquently testifies to the nondualistic understanding of reality, in which the two aspects of form and emptiness, universal and singular, personal and impersonal, and self and other coexist as one.

———————

We listen as our voice quiets down to the
soundless voice of a supreme love; and we
can listen with a selflessness that reaches
across the whole cosmos.

———————

One January day in 1982, I was wandering through the Sherman Oaks Guitar Center. As I was browsing through instruments I heard a sound that stopped me in my tracks: Coltrane. As I said, Coltrane's sound, though universal, was at the same time unique, one of a kind. I looked around and finally spotted a young African American kid playing an electronic saxophone. His phrasing was tentative, and he stumbled over some of the notes. But the sound and the soul were unmistakably Coltrane. I instinctively walked up to him. I said, "I've heard a lot of horn players, some great ones paying homage to Coltrane, but—this is the only time I've actually heard someone this close to the man himself." He smiled shyly and said, "Thank you." Then he went back to playing. I started to walk away but then turned back. I had to ask him his name. He said it was Ravi Coltrane—John's son.

When we meditate, if we're really focused, we listen to our voice and we smile. And then we can listen to the silence behind the voice, to the deep, boundless eternal stillness that underlies all our life. We listen as our voice quiets down to the soundless voice of a supreme love; and we can listen with a selflessness that reaches across the whole cosmos.

KEY STEPS IN YOUR PRACTICE:
A DAY OF MINDFULNESS

According to Genesis, after God created the world in six days an additional day was created for the purpose of peaceful rest and contemplation. Just as the rest notations in a musical score play a vital part in the music, so are the rests in our work schedules a critical part of our psychological balance and emotional well-being. Most religious traditions have recognized this fact and observe a day, such as the Sabbath, when normal activity is suspended; the mundane is transcended with communal prayer and quiet contemplation. In certain Eastern traditions that emphasize the transformation of consciousness, a Day of Mindfulness is similarly set aside.

Most of us have at least one day a week when we don't have to work. That can be a day of mindfulness. More time can be carved out during that day to practice mindful meditation. If you are normally practicing only once, maybe you can practice for two or three times during that day. Or maybe you can stretch out your usual sitting time. If you're used to sitting for twenty minutes, experiment with sitting for thirty to forty-five minutes. The day of mindfulness is a great opportunity to explore the experience of mindfulness and concentration. Since it is also a day that is freer of the usual pressures and anxieties of work, it could be a friendlier time to sit in calm focus. You can set a calming and harmonious tone with an early meditation, then continue a peaceful, compassionate awareness for the rest of the day. It can be a day when you exercise your mindfulness muscles for longer periods of time, maintaining a more consistent awareness of the present reality from moment to moment. You will find that observing a Day of Mindfulness can not only help your practice but also bring great joy and harmony and uplift to your whole life.

TECHNIQUES

Tonal Breath Meditation: Introduction

Normally the plain sound made by the breath has hardly any tonal or harmonic value. In tonal breath meditation we give the sound of the breath distinct pitches. Now we can follow the breath as a fully realized musical experience, listening with the same acute interest to the quality and tone of our present moment as we would listen to any musical performance. By mindfully combining tones with breathing, we become the sole performer and the sole audience, performing the breath and listening to the breath. Our mind and body are integrated into one instrument of receptive awareness.

Why add notes to the counting of the breath? Layering notes on top of numbers makes them sticky; the tones help cement your concentration on the breath. Combining a simple musical element that synchronizes with the count can effectively amplify the centrality of the breath as an object of attention. Blending music with numbers is similar to blending music with words. When melody underpins lyrics, the music acts as a mnemonic device, bracing the impact of the words. From jingles to pop songs, that principle has been put to work creating catchy hooks and "ear worms." That is why you can remember countless lyrics from songs and far fewer verses from poems. That is also why the great ancient works of literature before the printing press, such as the Torah, the Quran, Homer's *Odyssey* and *Iliad*, and Confucius's *Odes* were put to music. These epic works could be recited by heart because their words were laced with melody and therefore made memorable.

Our mind and body are

integrated into one instrument

of receptive awareness.

Singers can reshape the breathing apparatus into a beautiful wind instrument by engaging the vocal cords. This practice transforms the breath into a deep inner music by engaging the mind.

Indeed, there are many similarities between the concentration a musician has while producing their tones, via the voice or an instrument in performance, and tonal breath meditation. But there are also important differences. In a performance the musician is usually producing tonal sounds that are physical waves vibrating in space. A physical instrument of one kind or another, including vocal cords, is producing the sound created by the performer, and the musician and audience experience the sound or music through listening. During this meditation practice, however, the tonal aspect of the sound is being produced by and in the mind only. The breath is producing the pure sound, but the tonal quality we hear is solely in our minds.

While expressing the tonal breaths, remember to expand the abdomen and raise the diaphragm on the inhalation and contract the belly and lower the diaphragm on the exhalation. You can imagine an accordion expanding, filling with air and expressing a chord as your abdomen expands, and then the contraction and chord being voiced as you exhale. Or imagine a gust of wind glancing over an aeolian harp as you breathe, causing the strings on the harp to resonate harmonically.

Hopefully, when beginning this practice you can find a space quiet enough so that you can clearly hear your own breathing. Of course there will always be ambient sounds within your peripheral awareness. You can acknowledge these other sounds as part of the field of your attention. We know that in developing mindfulness and insight, the noting of environmental sounds is a well-established technique. But tonal breath meditation is a more specifically concentrative method that requires maintaining attention on the breath. When you turn again to the sound of your breathing, these other sounds may remain within the scope of your awareness, but your breathing will be the predominant object of attention—much like the vocalist in a band or the soloist in a concerto will be the central attraction, even though the other players are making music as well.

A good guideline for meditative practice in general is to keep it simple. Take for example Yves Klein's *Monotone-Silence Symphony* (1949), which consists of one chord being played for twenty minutes followed by twenty minutes of silence. In the simplicity of the one chord and its resonating silence, we approach the timeless and eternal stillness that underlies our impermanence. The less harmonic movement that we produce and hear, the more tranquil and still we can be—and the closer we can get to the unmovable ground of being.

Basic Tonal Breath Meditation

When we sit in tonal breath meditation, we hear a tone in our minds emitting with the sound of the breath. At the most basic level we hear a sustained tone that lasts as long as the in-breath, and again we hear a tone that sustains with the sound of the out-breath. The in-breath and out-breath may have the same tone, or they may sound two different tones.

Begin by "tuning the drum" (page 41). As you breathe, move your awareness through your body from your head to your toes. Notice any areas of tension. Calmly breathe with the area that is tense. If there is tightness, loosen it. Spend a few minutes with your mind-body tuning.

Now as you inhale, hear a tone or note with the sound of the breath. It can be any note.

After the inhalation, rest for a few seconds and then exhale. Again, as you exhale, hear a tone with the sound of the breath. It can be the same tone or a different tone. Remember, you are hearing the inhalation making a single note, holding at the top of the inhalation for a second or two and then exhaling while hearing the breath sound a single, sustained note.

The key is to keep the musical element very simple. Sustain a drone-like single tone throughout the inhalation, stop for a second or two, and then begin again to sustain a single tone during the exhalation. You can have the exhalation sound a different tone than the inhalation. It may be natural to use the same tone for all the inhalations and also a consistent tone—whether the same or different tone as the one for the inhalations—for all the exhalations.

If the tones shift after a while, however, that's perfectly fine. Whatever tone you happen to hear in the sound of your breath is the perfect tone. Whatever fluctuations or modulations you may hear in the tonality of your breathing are ideal because your experience is requiring those permutations at this moment. To quote Thelonious Monk again, "There are no wrong notes." Remember to keep the attention on the breath, the sounds, and tones without judging or analyzing. These are simple patterns being used as aids for concentration and wakefulness, not concert performances.

As our practice develops, we will vary the tones or chords we hear, both harmonically and rhythmically. The techniques will get a bit more intricate. Variety and novelty are useful to this practice, as they are to most endeavors. But the simpler the better, as the more complicated it gets the more our awareness is vulnerable to analysis and distraction. It's important not to overcomplicate the harmonic and rhythmic character of our breathing. If we get too intellectually involved, we may lose our essential focus. Until we can maintain undistracted concentration for a significant period, keep the pattern effortlessly basic.

Tonal Breath Meditation and Time Stretching

Another basic method of tonal breath meditation is to combine it with the simple counting and tempo elasticity used in time stretching.

In the first time stretching technique (page 70), you slowly stretched out the word *one* so that it lasted as long as the inhalation as you listened to the breath and the word. And again while exhaling, you elongated the silently sounded number *one* so it lasted as long as the exhalation. Now you will simply sing the numbers using your inner voice. Layer a single tone or note with the number you generate in your mind as you inhale and exhale. Instead of saying "one" tonelessly, you will sing it silently in sync with the breath. Sing "one" breathing in, and sing "one" again while breathing out. Any pitch or note that pops up with the number is the right pitch for that moment. Concentrate on the sound of the breath and the inner sound of the numbers as they go together. Count to either to ten or twenty-one and repeat.

Alternatively, you can sing the words *in* and *out*. When you sing the number in your head, say, "One, in" on the in-breath, "One, out," on the out-breath. Stretch out the words *in* and *out* so they last as long as the inhalation or exhalation. Count your breaths from one to ten and then count backward ten to one.

You can choose one or both of these methods or alternate them. Remember to pause in between the breaths and to listen to the silence between them. If at any time you feel short of breath, just go back to breathing at a normal pace. It's natural to want to pause the time stretch to "catch your breath." Once you feel comfortable in resuming, you can go back to the time stretch.

Remember that when you focus on the breath, the rhythm of the breathing will naturally slow down as the inhalations and exhalations deepen. The number sounded in the mind should keep time with this slower tempo. Keep the number you silently sing contemporaneous with the breathing; it will smooth the way for a peaceful, concentrated, and harmonious experience.

9.

Trance, Music, and Meditation

A FRIEND OF MINE, WHOM I was trying to introduce to meditation, wrote to me that he decided that he was already a meditator. When he listened to music it put him in a quiet and peaceful state of mind. To him, that was all the meditation he needed.

———

Meditation can make you feel like you're plugging into the same universal force that is behind the hurtling of planets through their orbits and the steady rhythmic beating of your heart.

———

Now it's true that both music and meditation can make one feel at ease, relaxed, blissfully peaceful, and calm. But while being captivated by music can be a trance or dream state, meditation is a path to a state of supreme wakefulness. And in contemplative states you can be very relaxed and calm, but at the same time you can be powerfully energized by the constant surging of pure being and pure awareness. Mindful meditation can arouse the same qualities of tranquility and equanimity that music can provide *plus* a clarity, stability, and expansiveness of awareness. It's both calming *and* energizing. Meditation can make you feel like you're plugging into the same universal force that is behind the hurtling of planets through their orbits and the steady rhythmic beating of your heart.

From the middle of the twentieth century until today, there have been composers who have written music designed to help cultivate mindfulness. Starting with John Cage and Luigi Russolo, these musicians have used their soundscapes to arouse the audiences' awareness of its sonic environment and the silence that pervades it. Their compositions are nonverbal guided meditations that seek to lead listeners to a heightened consciousness of how they *listen*. Some of these musical works are quite convincing as effective ways to develop mindfulness as the listener concentrates on the transitory path of sound waves and becomes more attentive to the process of awareness itself (we will go into these compositions in greater detail in the section "Composers of Silence and the Beautiful Mind," page 190). Much of this music is stunningly beautiful and revelatory on its own terms.

And some of these compositions have transformed the way musicians and audiences perceive not only sound but the whole of space and time. Yet though these works can be helpful additions to a repertoire of mindful training techniques, they have important limitations; they depend on an enforced regimen of sound patterns and restricted access to natural silence (with the exception of Cage's "indeterminate" compositions). The unfettered ability to hear one's own inner music as it naturally and spontaneously unfolds is too much at the heart of meditation to completely surrender.

Music can be a bridge to
that profound place,
but it is not that place.

It is possible for music to be a bridge between diffuse concentration and focused awareness and a bridge between an agitated mind and a relaxed mind. But then there is another bridge to a higher level of awareness, a connection to reality that transcends the personal, ego-centered agenda. As beautiful and tranquil as listening to music can be, in the end it still tethers consciousness to a self-referential framework, constricted by its reliance on sensory perceptions and reflections. In a higher state of relaxed awareness, consciousness is completely free from the limitations of sensory perception. It is unbounded by identity or agendas of the personal self. It drops you into a field of energy consciousness that seems to have no boundaries—one that allows for all things to happen without interference.

Since all sound is vibration, music is a disturbance in the environment. The path of meditation leads us deep beneath the disturbance to a place of profound stillness, beyond movement, beyond sound and silence. Music can be a bridge to that profound place, but it is not that place. Once you've been to that place, though, and brushed up against the mystery, when you return and hear music again you can experience it in an astonishingly and sublimely different way.

Inner Sound, Inner Silence

Listening to the inner sound with meditative mindfulness has been a leitmotif of this guide. We've been listening to a spontaneous, organic music that can only be heard with our internal ears: music that often begins with the sound of our breath resonating with the sounds of our surroundings and that trails off to resolve in silent clarity, profound calmness, and enhanced insight. We've been refining the art of listening to the point of being able to hear seven-part harmony in the scale of a single breath.

Listening to "external" music performed by musicians in the conventional sense has a different role to play. It can tone down an overactive mind and help it settle into a state of concentrated absorption. It can make one feel at ease, relaxed, blissfully peaceful, and calm. And these are all states that we are also cultivating through meditation and mindfulness—which is one reason we are often trying to make the meditative experience as musical as possible.

If a practitioner is having a particularly difficult time de-stressing and can't focus for more than a few seconds, it may be useful to listen to music to ease into it—as long as the music chosen doesn't provide additional distraction but rather helps quiet the mind and bring about more ease and relaxation. I went through tense phases in my life when listening to mallet-based instrumental music was conducive to calming my mind. I would listen during my second daily sitting, which was in the evening. Sometimes I would listen to recorded natural sounds such as birdsong. In either case, listening to entrancing, external stimuli put me in a more reflective mood for meditation.

The goal is to rely less on listening to music from the outside and to learn to rely more on the kind of music that plays silently from within.

It's best to use listening to music as a prelude to meditation. It can be a good way to settle the mind at the end of a day if you're mind just won't stop buzzing. Once its calming effect takes hold, you can turn off the music and move on to another mode of awareness. In general, silent sitting is still the most dependable method for refining both concentration *and* mindfulness, relaxation *and* wakefulness. The goal is to rely less on listening to music from the outside and to learn to rely more on the kind of music that plays silently from within.

Performing Music

As with listening to music, there are many parallels between performing music and meditative mindfulness. Both involve intense concentration, feelings of contentment, emotional release, transcendence, and harmony. And they both rely on extended periods of determined but relaxed, undistracted focus. We will explore in more detail in the next section these commonalities and how the practice of mindful meditation can enhance the musician's ability to perform. But first I want to underscore some important differences—primarily, how concentrated attention in the performance of music would be hard pressed to lead to a liberated and purely receptive awareness as can naturally occur during mindful meditation.

While performing the musician has to stick with the program. You can't waver from what the music needs you to do. Well, I suppose you could, but that would get you fired from the orchestra or band. Imagine you're the drummer or the bass player holding down the groove and you suddenly widen your focus on playing and open yourself up mindfully to the whole of your experience. Losing the beat and throwing the band into chaos could be the least of your problems.

The path of meditation—unlike the path of performing music—leads us deep beneath the roiling surface of sensory activity to a place of profound stillness, beyond movement, beyond sound, and beyond silence.

There is one other shortcoming. To calm and still the mind, it is best to keep the body still. As the body goes, so goes the mind. That is why we aim to sit motionless when we meditate. Performing music is very different in this respect; when you perform, you're in a state of constant activity. As a result, performing music and meditating produce different outcomes. When you can still the activities of the mind and body, you can allow another state of consciousness to come forward. It is very difficult to be alert to the stillness and silence at the heart of things when the mind and body are in constant flux. The path of meditation—unlike the path of performing music—leads us deep beneath the roiling surface of sensory activity to a place of profound stillness, beyond movement, beyond sound, and beyond silence.

Mindfulness and Meditation Can Make You a Better Musician

Almost all of the skills, habits, qualities, and developed innate capabilities that we've discussed as being transferrable from music to mindfulness can also go in the other direction. For example, meditation can sharpen concentration, and having greater powers of concentration is also helpful for a musician. Also, awareness training develops embodied cognition and the capacity of letting go of trying to control everything through mental dominance. It encourages seamless, harmonic cooperation among body, mind, and soul—which can enhance musical performance at any level.

Here are some more transferrable virtues from mindfulness to musical performance:

Patience and Perseverance: Musical life depends on the steadfastness to endure suffering and defeat. It calls upon the ability to persevere through hard times: through humiliation, frustration, boredom, and disappointment. Both disciplines rely on, and in turn bolster, patience and perseverance. These qualities can continue to be enhanced and refined as they pass back and forth between the two practices.

Disciplined Practice: Both practices require a level of disciplined time management. They depend on the commitment to carve out sections of a day for practice.

For those whose ability to stick with a consistent practice routine is fragile, mindful meditation practice might prove useful in overcoming that weakness.

Mindful Listening: Musical minds are generally good at listening. Especially in the meditation methods that we emphasize here, the art of listening is constantly being refined and cultivated. Mindful listening can play a big part in a musician's continuing creativity and development.

Creativity: Meditation and mindfulness refine many qualities that are helpful to creativity. Strengthening the connection to the intuitive faculty is one of them. Improving focus, discernment, nonjudgmental observation, mindful listening, patience, perseverance, and the art of letting go can all spur creativity and can all improve with awareness practice.

Transcending the Self: Music and meditation are both transcendent experiences that can lift the practitioner from the narrow constraints of identity. You can lose yourself in music just as you can let go of yourself in meditation. The liberation from egocentric habits and preconceptions generated by enhanced awareness can also free up creative energies for making music.

Compassion: Mindfulness increases self-compassion, compassion for others, and kindness. Self-compassion is important in creativity and performance because it dispels overly critical self-judgment. Compassion for others is an integral part of good leadership and the ability to play (music) well with others. And compassion fine-tunes the capacity for sympathetic vibrations.

Composure: Concentration and awareness practice can cultivate positive qualities such as equanimity, peacefulness, composure, harmony, and compassion. These are useful capabilities for dealing with the discord and cacophony that musicians often encounter. These are handy lifelong coping skills. These qualities will also prod you toward becoming a better human being, not just a better musician.

KEY STEPS IN YOUR PRACTICE: INSPIRATION

A professional songwriter or composer doesn't hang around waiting for inspiration to hit before sitting down to create. The composer treats creativity as an occupation and tries to keep a steady and consistent composing schedule. Inspiration comes with the writing. The routine is followed no matter the mood or the weather. Some days the creative work may be plodding and painstaking; on other days creativity might be flowing and euphoric. I've read that many published novelists maintain the same attitude. They routinely set aside time to write on every business day: Writing is their job, after all, not just a craft. First write, then the inspiration will come.

Meditation is much the same. We follow a routine, come rain or shine. We sit down to quiet the mind and watch what happens. The day may come while you're meditating that you have an extraordinarily inspiring experience. You may find yourself standing on the threshold of an amazing discovery. Or you may find yourself gazing with your whole being into the reality beyond existence and nonexistence. A sudden insight may totally shake up all your beliefs and ideas about life. It may profoundly change the way you see the world forever.

Usually when that happens we try to have the same experience again. Naturally we would want to repeat an extraordinary state of awakened consciousness or joyful discovery. Yet every meditation teacher maintains that those experiences almost never repeat themselves the same way. One shouldn't expect the same extraordinary experience to unfold again in the same manner. The advice they give is to keep the routine, maintain the steady practice of sitting down to work, just like the songwriter does. Other similar but different discoveries may or may not arise; just be patient. Maintain your relaxed and receptive awareness to whatever happens. Be patient in the pursuit of your practice. It may take a different form, but if inspiration has visited once, you can trust it will come again.

TECHNIQUES

Tonal Breath Meditation and the Performing Musician

There are many similarities between tonal breath meditation practice and musical performance. In a performance, the musician is highly focused on producing sound while simultaneously monitoring the sound she is producing. The intensity of concentration on the production of sound is at a very high level, assuming the musician is serious about the performance. The musician is almost completely immersed—body, mind, and soul—and is a producer and listener, the subject and the object at once. So this experience and ability of the musician to sustain a high degree of concentration and become integrated with the moment is a wonderful foundation for meditation practice.

Our meditation, however, is more like a silent, internal performance we put on for our own enjoyment and enlightenment. Someone sitting next to us may hear the breath, but they will be unable to hear the tone or chord that we are hearing. The fact is that the music is being produced, listened to, and experienced totally in the mind. Since we are conscious moment to moment that the whole show is only happening in the mind, it helps to bring us to a more limitless state of clear, undistracted awareness.

In addition, during a musical performance we focus on more than one thing. If we are playing with other musicians, we are aware of their positions and movements and what they are playing. We are interacting with them. If we are performing solo, our awareness extends outside our performance to encompass the audience. We wonder about their reactions, their level of involvement and receptivity. We worry about our appearance, our movements and how we sound out there. We also plan our next moves or think about the next song on the set list. By contrast, during meditation we have none of these potential distractions. We focus fully on the here and now.

Alternating between tone and tonelessness, and coordinating the character, quality, tempo, and duration of tone and toneless sound with our breathing, is essential to this practice. The length of the tone or toneless phases can be determined spontaneously. Breathing for five or ten or any number of counts during a sequence is arbitrary. Once you establish a rhythm and are generally in a focused meditative state, you can improvise as to how long the phases are sustained. Like improvising a jazz performance, you can work within the boundaries we set forth to modify the practice to whatever is working at the moment. If it all is flowing one way, just go with it.

Counting Tonal Beats and Bars

We've already learned how to count the four phases of the breath as a four-bar phrase. We've also learned how to combine tones with basic breath concentration. Now we can simply combine tones with the counting-beats method to give our meditation more color and texture.

Remember that in rhythmic breath counting, each phase of breathing is treated as one discrete bar with four beats—in 4/4 time. We've been counting the inhalation for four beats, then holding the breath for four beats, then counting the exhalation for four beats, and finally holding the end of the exhalation for four beats. Before, the numbers were simply counted tonelessly with our inner voice. Now we will combine a tone with each beat that we count. In effect, each beat will be heard internally as a pitched quarter note; each beat is sung instead of spoken.

Here's a basic example of a tonal pattern I use: For the first two bars I hear the same note on each counted beat for the first three beats and then add a note that is a whole step above for the fourth beat. During the second two-bar phrase on the exhalation and hold, I just keep the same note for all four quarter notes (a quarter note here can be as long as four seconds plus) looking like this:

Inhalation	Hold	Exhalation	Hold
do do do re	do do do re	do do do do	do do do do
1 2 3 4	1 2 3 4	1 2 3 4	1 2 3 4

Continuing to the second breath, counting would follow the same numbering pattern—and standard musical practice—as the nontonal method:

do do do re   do do do re   do do do do   do do do do
2 2 3 4   2 2 3 4   2 2 3 4   2 2 3 4

You can generate tones in any interval configuration that pops into your mind. It's best to keep it natural and spontaneous, so that your focus stays undividedly on the count and the breath. That's why I use the simple patterns I've explained as a basis for tonal counting. The tones are there to act as an aid to concentration, not a distraction. It's also important to remember that there is no rigid tempo, and that time stretching is natural.

Try this method counting from one to ten (or twelve, like a twelve-bar blues). Of course you can stop at any time that you feel you need to catch your breath. If you can continue after one cycle, go for a few more and then go back to breathing naturally. No counting or holding. Simply follow the breath by listening and watching your mind and body. Then repeat.

Counting Tonal Beats and Resonant Silence

Once you lay down a good groove of tonal breath counting, you can transition into states of mindful noticing. Depending on how you feel at the time, you can either alternate between the two states or stay in open awareness.

At the end of a few ten- or twelve-bar cycles, stop the tonal counting and pair your breath with words: On your inhalation, silently say "listening." On your exhalation, silently say "watching." When you say "listening," listen to your experience of listening. When you say "watching," observe your experience and your state of mind.

After some time drop the word "watching" so that you only say "listening."

Inhalation: "Listening"
Exhalation: *Silence* (just listen and observe)

The next phase is to drop words altogether. Breathe and observe the goings-on in your mind. If your attention is settled and you are comfortable lingering here, please do so. You can stay with the open awareness of whatever falls into your field of experience. If you feel that your mind still needs more composure, you can return to your tonal breath counting.

You have no thoughts, no personal stake in anything, no sense of a defined self with any attributes.

If you do continue in silent observation you may reach a point where everything falls away except for the simple and pure reality of your own existence. You have no thoughts, no personal stake in anything, no sense of a defined self with any attributes. It's as if the total sum of what you are and the essence of who you are have nothing to do with your personality, memory, status, feelings, achievements, failures—whatever you perceive as your identity. Your only identity is pure *being* itself. Now you see that your own existence is always staring you in the face, but you look past it. You never see it, just like you can never see your own eyes—until a cleansing of awareness casts a reflection and everything changes.

10.

Sympathetic Vibrations

SOMETIME IN THE EARLY 1970s, when I was a college student, I had the singular experience of spending some intimate time with the celebrated American poet and founding beatnik Allen Ginsberg. My good friend Amram Shapiro was the host of a literary radio program at Columbia University. Ginsberg had agreed to come back to his alma mater to perform some of his poetry for a student audience to be broadcast on Amram's show. A female punk band called Flaming Youth was his opening act. Amram must have talked up my lyrics because Ginsberg invited me back to his tiny apartment on the Lower East Side where he lived with his companion, Peter Orlovsky.

At first we hung out in his small living room that was strewn with the sleeping bags of the band. I was really looking forward to playing for him, as I was hoping that he would be sufficiently impressed to introduce me to his brother-in-arms and my role model, Bob Dylan. At some point he invited me into his modest book-lined study, where he sat on the floor. I sat on a chair so that I could play guitar while I sang. He allowed me one song, which he listened to intently. To my disappointment he didn't declare me to be the natural heir to Dylan.* When it was his turn he brought out a very small, accordion-like instrument called a harmonium, which was given to him in India. I can't recall exactly what it was that he chanted while accompanying himself on the harmonium. Whatever it was, he chanted in a pleasantly strong voice that made up in passion and soul what it lacked in melodic distinction.

After chanting, he asked me if I played the piano. I told him I did, and he proceeded to try to convince me that my familiarity with keyboards qualified me to teach him how to improve his abilities on the harmonium, since it also had a little keyboard. In the face of his eagerness to learn I was particularly disappointed that I had to demur. I had no idea how to work the harmonium's bellows, and I lacked confidence that my own piano skills could effectively transfer to this other medium.

But even these many years later, I am continuously struck by the intensity of Ginsberg's desire to learn that instrument. After all, he was a wordsmith in the Whitman mold. His poetry embraced the whole range of humanity, and he was widely celebrated for his transcendent spirit and exceptional largeness of

---

* He made one comment about an image in my lyrics, "to reveal a ring of ancient men sitting lotus around an opium lamp." He held that when smoking opium, you lie down.

heart and soul. Yet he still felt an emptiness that music, in the form of chanting thus far, needed to fill. Playing the harmonium was important to him, because it supported his chanting. For Ginsburg, chanting was not only an expression of his art but a sonic exploration with a profoundly spiritual and universal purpose. He believed that chanting connects the individual to the fundamental vibrations of the cosmos, and that if we can vibrate in tune with the cosmos we can realize our basic nature, which is in sympathy with everything else.

Sympathetic vibrations arise whenever two musicians play together with common intent. While producing their own unique sounds they nonetheless stay constantly attuned to each other through nonverbal perception and communication. This sonic communion has been embraced by almost every religion and spiritual practice. From hymns to chanting, Hindu mantras to Chassidic Jewish *niggunim*, reserved psalmody to exuberant gospel choirs, music brings unity and harmony to diverse communities. Even the average nonmusician knows the feeling of fulfillment, comfort, and interconnectedness in resonating sympathetically with others through the sound of music—whether rapping the lyrics in unison with the crowd in a hip-hop club, letting loose with friends at a karaoke bar, or singing the national anthem at a sporting event. We can build on these transpersonal experiences by practicing mindfulness to deepen and strengthen empathy and compassion for ourselves and for others.

Sympathetic vibrations arise whenever two musicians play together with common intent.

. . .

Some may even experience their own minds and bodies as vibrating waves, resonating in harmony with other waves.

Meditation goes even further, strengthening our capacity to feel the vibrations of others and deepening this sense of interconnectedness with *all beings.* We listen to the whole world with the same concentration and sensitivity with which we listen to the performers with whom we make music without judgment or identification. We can stay receptive to whatever sounds or silences unfold, inside or outside of us. Some may even experience their own minds and bodies as vibrating waves, resonating in harmony with other waves. As the mind and heart grow more receptive and selflessly attuned to the world, feelings of compassion and loving-kindness naturally develop.

A GANGSTA'S GRATITUDE

"Gratitude is not only the greatest of virtues but the
parent of all the others."—**Cicero**

"Nuthin' but a G thang . . ."—**Dr. Dre, Snoop Dogg**

The first thing my parents do when they wake up in the morning
is to stand in an embrace and express their gratitude. They've
been doing this every day for as long as I can remember. Maybe
they've found the elixir of youth—they are into their nineties
now and still mentally and physically vibrant.

The practices of mindfulness and gratitude are interleaved
like the left and right channels of a stereo bounce. One of the
outcomes of mindfulness is a new sense of wonder and awe for
much of what you usually take for granted. Everything you
encounter appears fresh and vibrant; ultimately you marvel
that the capacity of awareness itself is a great miracle. This
appreciation then often leads to pleasant feelings of gratitude
for this gift of life and consciousness and everything perceived
within it.

The practice of gratitude can bring many rewards. There
is in fact a field of research that studies the neuroscience of
gratitude and has identified some of its benefits. Leaders in
the "science of gratitude" such as Dr. Robert Emmons of the

University of California, Davis, and Dr. Glenn Fox of the University of Southern California's Performance Science Institute have amassed a body of data supporting the view that gratitude can add quantifiable value to physical and mental health. Their research concludes that the practice of thankfulness not only leads to lower blood pressure, a stronger immune system, and an extended life span but is also the best predictor of feelings of well-being.

There was never more compelling testimony of the power of gratitude to spread joy than what I witnessed one night between two musicians in a steamy hip-hop club in downtown LA.

It was the middle of winter in 1993 and I had been in the studio producing the boy band sensation New Kids on the Block. Donnie Wahlberg, the lead rapper of the band, was hanging out after finishing some vocal overdubs and he suggested we go down to Glam Slam, Prince's hot hip-hop club. Going to Glam Slam was always a trip, as it was filled with die-hard hip-hop heads, gangbangers, pop music fans, college students, and notable hip-hop or R&B artists who happened to be passing through town. It was a winning proposition.

That night the DJ was the super producer Dr. Dre. Dre's solo debut album *The Chronic* had come out at the end of 1992, and by then it was dominating not only hip-hop and R&B, but it seemed to be reigning over the entire pop landscape. Without sacrificing his provocative and rebellious edge, Dre had extended hip-hop's influence beyond urban radio to the culture at large.

Donnie and I were hanging out in the back of the club when Dre finished his set. As he came off the stage he was intercepted by various well-wishers and groupies. Even though he was making only halting progress through the club, it seemed that he was aiming his body in our direction. Sure enough, his trajectory toward us was deliberate, and he was clearly walking with a purpose.

Dre is a big guy, especially compared to Donnie and me, and as his imposing bulk drew nearer I felt a mix of anticipation and mystification. What did this incredibly brilliant producer and notorious promoter of hard-core gangsta rap want with us? He didn't know me, and Donnie was a fading heartthrob outgrowing his well-scrubbed white boy pop band.

But as he stopped in front of us I could see that he knew Donnie and that his intentions were nothing but friendly. As he spoke to Donnie his face radiated warmth and appreciation, and as he had to bow his head to reach our level, it gave an impression of great respect and deference. The loudness of the club made it difficult to hear what he was saying, but you could easily discern the thankfulness in his tone and body language. Here was this looming figure at the height of influence, popularity, and relevance, with a notorious reputation for his aggressive attitude and gangster ties, humbly showing his sincere gratitude. I watched incredulously as the two seemed locked in some kind of secret beatific embrace. As Dre expressed his parting thanks and walked away, he was still beaming with pleasure.

As soon as we were alone again, I asked Donnie to explain what had just happened. Much of what he told me was unexpected, but at the same time it made total sense. Donnie had a production deal with the legendary record mogul Jimmy Iovine at Interscope Records, and he had brought them desperately needed success with his brother Mark Wahlberg's hip-hop group, Marky Mark and the Funky Bunch. The two Top 10 singles and certified platinum album that Donnie produced helped save the label from bankruptcy. In the meantime, Dre split from N.W.A. and his highly gifted partner Eazy-E's Ruthless Records, and he holed up in the studio to independently record *The Chronic*. He and manager Suge Knight then pounded the pavements in New York and LA looking for a distributor, but everyone shut them out, fearing a backlash against the glorified violence and misogyny of gangsta rap. When the project landed in front of Jimmy Iovine, he was undeterred by any consideration other than its commercial viability. Jimmy admittedly had scant knowledge about hip-hop, so he did what any clever executive would do—he sought the advice of trusted business partners who did know the genre. So naturally he turned to Donnie for his take. Donnie told him, in the most emphatic way possible, that if he let Dr. Dre walk without signing him he would regret it every day for the rest of his life. So Iovine ended up signing Dre and Death Row Records. Shortly thereafter, while Dre was on the way to the celestial heights of five times certified platinum, Iovine let Donnie's deal drift through the ozone hole in the record biz into pop star oblivion. (Donnie Wahlberg did, of course, go on to a highly successful career acting in film and television.)

Dr. Dre, at the peak of power and popularity, could have lived up to the overweening pride of anyone in his position. After all, the critics, fans, DJs, and radio programmers were all glad-handing him and praising his indomitable gifts. Yet he had the grace to humbly express his debt to another person for aiding his success. And the way Dre was buoyed by the encounter proved that signaling feelings of sincere gratitude can reverberate back waves of contentment. He showed that gratitude may be a greater gift to the giver than it is to the receiver.

KEY STEPS IN YOUR PRACTICE:
TAKE 5/4 MINDFULNESS

Back in the days of analog recording of large ensembles of union musicians, it used to be quite common for the producer or band leader at a session to periodically tell the musicians to "take five" (in today's digital studio environment, where it's mostly just a few nonunion musicians, that expression is less widespread).* It was a union requirement that the players would have the right to take a "breather" from the recording: to take some time out and clear their minds. Then presumably after the break they could come back refreshed and energized to continue the session.

We can look for opportunities during the day's business to "take five" for a few minutes of mindfulness. We can create openings to press the pause button and calmly tune in to the reality of what is happening right now. We can create the space to compose ourselves and consciously connect to our breathing and to the whole of our experience.

For example, as you close a door you can give your whole attention to the slow and calm movement of closing the door. When you start walking you can be mindful of your breath, the feeling of the ground beneath your feet, and the movements of your body. You can maintain that heightened awareness and clarity of mind as you walk to wherever you are going. You

---

* The classic hit "Take Five" made world-famous by Dave Brubeck is in 5/4 time.

are in effect "taking five" from your normal stress responses to refresh yourself in a peaceful stream of receptive awareness.

You may find that there are typically mundane circumstances that afford you opportunities to cultivate mindfulness. Maybe you're stuck in bumper-to-bumper rush hour traffic and your natural response of anger and frustration is building to a head. What a perfect opportunity to "take five" for mindfulness. You can turn your attention toward your feelings of anger and frustration. By acknowledging those feelings, you will be creating space around them and they will lose their potency to captivate your emotions. No longer caught up in stressful and anxious feelings, you can relax into an awareness of your breathing. You can take a "breather" and actually find joy in the consciousness that you are alive and aware in this moment.

We can create the space to
compose ourselves and consciously
connect to our breathing and
to the whole of our experience.

There can be many other opportunities to mindfully "take five." You can be fully present when you wait for the light to cross the street, walk the dog, turn on your phone, wash your hands, drink your coffee, or open a MIDI file. Anytime you are involved in an activity and your attention is totally engaged *and you know that it is engaged*, you can be mindful.

Sitting down to eat is a common activity that many use to practice mindfulness. In some contemplative communities the participants eat their meals in communal silence (called "noble silence"), so that they can devote their whole consciousness to experiencing the food and all the physical processes involved in eating it. They count every chew; pay close attention to where the food is in relation to the teeth; notice the texture, taste, and flavor of the food, the position of the tongue, and the sounds in the room; and so on. Incidentally, being wholly conscious of the experience of eating while you eat is not only a great training ground for strengthening mindfulness but also—fortunately—a great way to improve your digestion and maintain healthy weight.

As your powers of concentration, awareness, and presence develop, you will find yourself responding to stressful situations in a more relaxed, clear, and even manner. Of course you will still feel fear, irritation, shock, frustration, and anxiety; but with practice these feelings will have less potency and permanence. You will enjoy an improved ability to assess your situation with greater perspective and clarity. You meet your experiences with more understanding, self- compassion, and compassion for others. And though your stress responses will still give voice to negative thoughts and emotions, the love song that is always playing in your heart will be just a few decibels louder.

TECHNIQUE: HEALING BREATH MEDITATION— A MINIMALIST COMPOSITION

Here is a very simple but very potent meditation. Because it speaks of the breath and is so effortless to express, after a short while the words flow naturally of themselves. There is no need to think of anything else or for the mind to travel anywhere else.

Focus your mind on the wind in your nostrils. When you exhale, alternate between pushing the air out with different degrees of force. In any case, try to keep attention on the nostrils, the airflow, and the sentence.

In-breath: *Every breath is a healing breath,*
Out-breath: *and I'm so grateful.*

When the breath slows, the meter of the words may sound like this:

In-breath: *Ev-e-ry breath*
is-a heal-ing-breath,

Out-breath: *and I'm-*
so-
grateful.

Also try to pause, if only briefly, at the end of the inhalation before starting the exhalation.

After a while you can subtly substitute some of the words. Keep the same rhythmic pattern and division between the in-breath and out-breath:

Ev-e-ry breath
is a
bliss-ful-breath
and I'm
so
grateful.

Just like the "The Little Refrain" (page 111), one of the great virtues of this meditation is its portability. You can use this simple meditation anytime throughout the day, in any situation: walking to the car, in between responding to emails, closing a door, looking at your smartphone. Just taking a few conscious breaths and saying "Every breath is a healing breath, and I'm so grateful" can bring you back to a state of calm and equanimity. It certainly has come in handy for me during some intense circumstances.

Whenever we feel gratitude for the ability to breathe and to be conscious, we are aware of the true dimension of reality. We are breathing from our magnanimous mind, freed from our clouded egotistical mind. And it reveals to us one of the great pleasures of peace.

Our minds often hunger for novelty. After all, since everything is impermanent in the relativistic universe, we are given to seeking change. So at times you may be in the mood to modify the healing breath. Here are some variations that you may enjoy.

The simplest one is to do a certain number of healing breaths and then alternate with a number of counting or noting breaths. For instance, you could do five healing breaths, then five noting breaths, then cycle back to the healing breaths, and repeat.

Say for five breaths:

Ev-e-ry breath
is a
bliss-ful-breath
and I'm
so
grateful.

Then say for five breaths:

I know I am breathing in
I know I am breathing out

Another variation you may enjoy is to substitute *healing* with other adjectives such as *calming, peaceful, joyful*, and so on.

Ev-e-ry breath
is a
peace-ful-*breath*
and I'm
so
grateful.

Or you can change the rhythm slightly again:

Ev-e-ry breath
*is **ha-ppi-ness***
and I'm
so
grateful.

Finally, you can alternate between the healing meditation and counting breaths. So at first you do five healing breaths and then count five silent breaths. Alternate the two techniques for as long as you like.

The shifts here are akin to a minimalist composition, in the mode of Philip Glass, Steve Reich, Terry Riley, and so on. You have a repeating riff or arpeggio pattern that after a certain number of cycles slightly shifts harmonically, melodically, or rhythmically. In this instance the words slightly shift as the sentence and breath continue to repeat.

11.

Transcending the Self

"Lose Yourself"—**Eminem**

WHEN BRUCE SPRINGSTEEN PUBLISHED HIS memoir, *Born to Run*, he was interviewed by *The New Yorker* and talked about how he had first turned to performing music as a vehicle for "self-erasure." It was so hard for him to live with himself, he said, but when performing he could disappear into his audience and "rise up and vanish" into the music.

Music and meditation are both transcendent experiences that can lift the practitioner from the prison of identity. They both provide an experience of liberation from the ordinary limitations defined by the ego to unite with something much greater than the self. It's an experience that can be deeply spiritual and bring profound calm and tranquility that come from letting go of the self. As Eminem famously advised, if you're serious about music, "lose your*self*" (italics mine). Losing yourself, or "letting go," is potentially one of the most transformative stages of mindfulness meditation. In the vein of Springsteen's vanishing act while performing on stage, many songwriters have said that they themselves could not claim responsibility for creating their songs; rather, they felt they were instruments of some greater power that was playing *them*. Bob Dylan has sung, "I don't write the song, the song writes me"; and Keith Richards wrote, the riff "plays you."

The experience of transcending the ego and losing the self in music extends to the listener as well as the creator. Composers and artists have the power to transport the listener to ecstatic states that many have described as an experience of union of the self with a higher power.

If music has this transcendental power on its own, why, then, do professional musicians who spend so much of their lives making and listening to music, from Paul McCartney and Kendrick Lamar to Philip Glass and Rick Rubin, still practice meditation? What is the affinity between the two, and what is the void that music alone does not fill?

Musical transcendence on its own lacks an important dimension. Even after having blissful, cathartic musical epiphanies, musicians still can feel emptiness. Although they love music with a timeless and immutable love, once the music stops, they can sense there is something still further beyond even the most selfless experience that music opens up for them. There exists a field of consciousness that they have yet to visit and that requires a different path to enter. Musicians have been known to experiment with drugs as a means to attaining these expansive states of consciousness. But others have instead found their way to meditation, mindfulness, and insight.

Whereas music is braided with the stuff of fantasy and dreams, mindfulness can lead to states of heightened wakefulness—greater attunement with reality itself. This is where these overlapping paths of self-transcendence diverge. Music may liberate you from the prison cell of your self for a short while; the door is opened, and the prisoner is taken outside and allowed to breathe the fresh air, to see the sun, to walk freely. But then the music stops; you're taken back to the cell, and the prison door shuts. In mindfulness you realize that the prison bars are not real. You can pass through them at will. As the ancient Zen expression goes, once you awaken to the truth, you can "freely pass through the gateless gate."

The Universal Drummer

It is said that one of our essential psychological needs is to feel that we have control over our lives. There is this basic, primal need for control. And when something happens that defies our intentions, we feel intense dissatisfaction. We suffer at the perceived loss of control. To save ourselves from some of the unnecessary frustrations caused by the illusion of control, it's probably a good thing to wake up and take a look at exactly what we do and don't control.

For instance, when you think about "your" body, how much control do "you"—the self who seemingly exists somewhere in the body and to whom the body belongs—have? Are you the only one in control of all the processes in your body, or are there also other influencers?

Now it's time to meet what we can call "the universal drummer." As a thought experiment, let's see what part the drummer plays in controlling your body every minute of the day. You don't beat your own heart; the universal drummer does. The universal drummer sets the tempo of your breathing until you tinker with it in meditation or other activities. And the universal drummer also dials in your circadian rhythms, sets the BPMs for pumping blood through your veins, drums up antibodies in the spleen, counts off the release of insulin by your pancreas, slaps together the spinal fluid to coat your brain, and cues the marrow in your bones to produce blood cells, as well as hosting many other physical festivities.

And this same universal drummer can pop up in all the unlikeliest places. That's why practitioners of meditative mindfulness refer to the "illusion of control." It's helpful to be at peace with this reality of our limited control, to be at ease with letting go of the need for control, to breathe a sigh of relief that it's actually a good thing that you can't have control. Because if you actually could take control away from the universal drummer, you'd probably be dead in short order.

Though we may not be able to control what happens to us, we *can* control our responses. We can look at what is happening calmly and clearly, without reacting to it and without piling on the frustration and dissatisfaction that comes with telling ourselves that we should be in control. When we frame potentially painful events mindfully, we can meet them with more distance, peace, and perspective. As Epictetus said, "Men are disturbed not by events but by their opinion of events."

———————

*Though we may not be able to control what happens to us, we **can** control our responses.*

———————

We have total control of our opinions, desires, aversions— the stories we tell ourselves. If we gratefully allow the universal drummer to control the rest, we'll be free to focus on the good beats and vibrations.

FLOAT LIKE A BUTTERFLY

We carry around this image of the mind as wedged between the bones of our skull. The steady streams of thoughts that weigh us down keep us there. The iron-fisted control of the Darwinian ego over our conscious awareness slices off a tiny sliver of consciousness within which we can barely roam. But through meditation we condition ourselves to expand the mind and its image beyond any boundaries. When the mind is calm and free floating, skipping like a rock across the surface of a lake or floating like a feather in the wind, it can appear to be anywhere.

POWER SITTING WITH UNIVERSAL AWARENESS

The concept of *insight meditation* may imply that there is something limited that only dwells within. A more descriptive term might be *insight-outsight meditation*. Because when we transcend our personal mind-body and experience a state of pure awareness, it is as if we are swimming in an ocean of boundless mind, the edges of which are unreachable. We are not only diving deeper into ourselves but also floating along with a powerful current that has a source outside the boundaries of our self and is expanding in every direction. We are electrified by a force that "surrounds all worlds and fills all worlds" (from the Kabbalistic text the *Tanya*). Even though we are tapping into this powerful energy of mindfulness, we are relaxed, peaceful, and calm. This paradox is possible because the ego is quiet and subdued, and we are simply part of a limitless state of being without feeling our self as a totally separate entity.

The state of pure awareness is accompanied by feelings of wonder and appreciation.

. . .

If you enjoy streaming music, you may grow to love streaming consciousness.

We can relate this paradox of being still and flowing at the same time to our current sitting posture. We are sitting extremely still on a chair or cushion, but at the same time we earthlings are hurtling through space at 1,000 miles per hour (460 meters per second) revolving around Earth's axis while orbiting the sun at about 66,000 mph (107,000 kilometers per hour). Our mind is still and calm, but at the same time it is flowing with the universal stream of awareness.

A Buddhist method encourages the meditator to observe the mind within the mind and the body within the body. There are differing interpretations, but for me this teaching expresses this very state of pure awareness. In this state we realize that our own consciousness is part of a larger consciousness (the mind within the mind) and that our physical body not only extends throughout the entire cosmos but is an extension or dimension of consciousness; it is a body of awareness. We can experience our bodies as pulsing with the fundamental energy that exists on the quantum level and that is in rhythm with all other bodies in the universe.

The state of pure awareness is accompanied by feelings of wonder and appreciation. As you're filled with this effulgent energy, you marvel at the miracles of your awareness and existence in this world. This state is called *satchitananda* in Hindu/Sanskrit texts: "pure being, pure consciousness, and bliss." Flowing freely with the strong undercurrents of meditative wakefulness has its unique delights. If you enjoy streaming music, you may grow to love streaming consciousness.

MYSTERY BALLROOM: KNOWING
THAT YOU DON'T KNOW

Although awareness may be limitless, we can ultimately go only so far. The landscape is always changing, so when we think we're nearing the horizon it just moves a little farther away from us. Mindfulness is not only knowing *that* you know but also knowing that you *don't* know.

The "don't know" mind is a receptive mind, a mind that still has the room to increase in insight and wisdom. When you know everything, you don't need to listen to another point of view. On the other hand, when you're aware that your understanding has limits, you can really listen to another person. You can completely tune in not only to what is said but also to what is unsaid.

*Mindfulness is not only knowing **that** you know but also knowing that you **don't** know.*

You can never go outside of your awareness to see what it really looks like, just like you can never look directly at your face—you can look at a piece of glass in front of your face, but that will only show you a reflection. There is no separation between us and our awareness, so we can never get outside of it in order to see it, just like we can never get outside our face in order to see it directly. Mindfulness is how we feel and experience our awareness, and also how we can observe its reflection in our lives. We are also mindful that there is an untouchable, invisible aspect to ourselves. It's more real than a reflection, and it continues to hang out there, an insoluble mystery. It allows us to see that there is still mystery behind what we think we know. It uncovers our pure "don't know" mind, which we entered this world with and which is fine-tuned to the wonders of life.

TECHNIQUE: SELF-INQUIRY—
THE SOUL METHOD

1. What's Going On? The Soul Method

"What's going on?"—**Marvin Gaye**

"You may ask yourself . . ."—**Talking Heads**

Since Marvin Gaye plaintively and persistently posed it in his now-classic soul lyric, the question "What's going on?" has reverberated with preternatural power throughout our collective consciousness. That memorable refrain is the basis of a simple, direct, and very effective method of self-inquiry that can bring about a state of deep concentration, penetrating insight, and lasting mindfulness.

Like all catchy choruses, this phrase also has a life of its own that makes it a very effective tool for staying concentrated first on your breath and then on the goings-on in the whole field of your awareness. Combining the rhythmic timing of the hook "What's going on?" with your inhalation unites two involuntary and autonomous activities—your breathing and a hook that keeps playing in your mind—to help anchor concentration. Whenever your attention wanders it will soon be pulled back by the persistent, clear question—"What's going on?"—as you take your next breath.

Besides being catchy and rhythmic, this particular hook has another transcendent virtue. It also directly serves the purpose of pointing your attention to the job at hand: observing your mind, without judging or getting tangled up in what you observe.

Self-inquiry of this type is a well-established mode of self-realization in various contemplative cultures. "What is my true self?" and "What is this?" are a few of the more famous inquiries to meditate on. In this variation we observe the unfolding of our awareness and ask ourselves, "What's going on?"

Begin as usual by "tuning the drum," calmly bringing your attention to the body.

Continue to relax and stabilize the body and mind for the next few minutes using a simple method such as counting and listening to the breath.

Now as you take a conscious in-breath, listen to your inner voice, silently asking: "What's going on?"

At the top of your inhale, pause and observe your mind: What is happening in your experience right now?

Whatever you observe happening, note it on the out-breath. So your answer might be "Watching my breath," or "Waiting for something to happen," or "Listening to the birds outside."

It's important to remember that you want to witness what is happening in your experience without dwelling on it. The practice is to note what is going on from an unbiased, non-judgmental, impersonal perspective. Try to keep your noting as simple and succinct as possible.

Some meditation teachers suggest that your noting should be truncated to one word. They refer to this method as "labeling." The answer to the question of what is happening might be "Thinking," "Listening," "Breathing," "Drifting," or "Nothing." You may find that you are just watching your breath and that your answer is repeatedly "Breathing." That means you are in a state of deep concentration and are likely feeling calm and peaceful, which is always a beautiful event.

You want to witness what is

happening in your experience

without dwelling on it.

In one process, thinking these four syllables—"What's going on?"—in sync with your breath accomplishes the attainment of both concentration and mindfulness. The insistent question keeps the focus on your body's breath and is a reminder to open the scope of your attention to the whole of your present experience.

Another way to first establish mental calmness is to combine "What's going on?" with breath counting. Start from any number you choose and start counting backward. After silently saying each number, ask "What's going on?" on the inhalation and answer the question on the exhalation. For example, if you count backward from ten you would say on the . . .

> In-breath: Ten, what's going on?
> Out-breath: Answer (*Remembering breakfast*)
> In-breath: Nine, what's going on?
> Out-breath: Answer (*Sitting in this chair*)
> And so on.

You can start from any number. Keep this up as long as you like. At any time, you can drop the count and continue with the inquiry.

2. What's Going On? All-Day Marvin Gaye

> "Self-inquiry is the one infallible means, the only direct one, to realize the unconditioned, absolute being that you really are."—**Sri Ramana Maharshi**

Mindfulness can be described as knowing what's happening as it's happening without adding anything: to be fully conscious of what's going on and the nuances of your response to what's going on. Mindfulness means having, as much as humanly possible, a clear, virtually undistorted view of the present reality that's unfolding in your mind, in your heart, in the totality of your experience.

During the course of an average day we can pop these questions to ourselves: What's going on? What's really happening? What's going on in my framing of reality? Am I seeing this clearly? Are my preconceptions distorting the truth of what is happening? Is my reaction to what is going on useful? Is it the best response? Am I really listening, really paying attention?

Marvin Gaye's words when turned around into self-inquiry can be a companion when we are off the cushion and not sitting in formal meditation. It can be a useful tool to keep us mindful throughout our daily lives. We may be in the middle of a tense situation or an impossible dilemma. Simply asking ourselves "what's going on?" can pull us back into relaxed awareness. Our attention will be drawn to our breath and to the quality of our cognitive process. Controlling our breath will smooth the way to controlling our mind. And with conscious awareness we can observe "what's going on" without egocentric discrimination and without getting entangled in thoughts or feelings. And that can help us maintain a composed, clear, and harmonious mental state in any circumstance.

3. What's Going On? A Sample Meditation

In this meditation, "What's going on?" is repeated on the inhalation; on the exhalation answers are improvised. There is no counting in this variation.

What's going on?
I'm sitting here.
What's going on?
I'm aware that I'm breathing.
What's going on?
Someone is asking what's going on.
What's going on?
Who wants to know?
What's going on?
I'm watching to see what happens.
What's going on?
I'm asking that myself.
What's going on?
I'm right here.
What's going on?
I'm getting very relaxed.
What's going on?
My breathing is very loud and slow.
What's going on?
A whole lot of stuff.
What's going on?
It's very peaceful and very still.
What's going on?
Still going on.

12.

Silence

"I had accepted the idea that the purpose of music is to sober and quiet the mind, thus making one susceptible to divine influences." —**John Cage**

WE'VE BEEN DISCUSSING FROM THE outset how musicians' sensitivity to silence can play a role that is hard to overestimate in developing a contemplative practice. In many of our meditative exercises we've underscored how practicable listening to the silences between sounds can be in composing and clarifying your mind. We've depended on your ability to attend deeply to the interplay between internal and external sound and silence as a key skill to tap while traveling along the meditative path. So it's no wonder why we're winding up here, facing the final bridge of silence.

This is how fundamentally important silence is to music: The universal system for writing music gives the same weight to a measure of silence as it does to a measure of sound. Accordingly, for every notation for the duration of a sound there is an equal notation for the duration of silence. A quarter note symbol for a rest balances a quarter note symbol for a tone; there are complimentary rest notations for long whole notes and short sixteenth notes—even down to a faster-than-a-speeding-bullet-train hemidemisemiquaver! (A hemidemisemiquaver, or sixty-fourth note, of silence is pretty much what most people experience in this socially networked era.)

So it's no wonder why we're winding up
here, facing the final bridge of silence.

Earlier, I brought up Miles Davis and how he unexpectedly enlightened me about the significance of silence. In his lecture series at Harvard University, the legendary jazz master Herbie Hancock, who was part of Miles's ensemble for many years, pointedly spoke about how Miles helped him uncover the connection between the role of silence in music and in life. He described how his mentor taught him that when he plays music he should evoke silence by listening to the notes that he could leave out. Hancock carried this insight into his everyday life. He believes that silence is not only a "vital component of

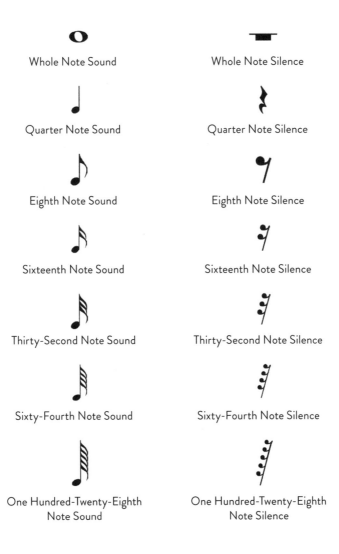

Whole Note Sound

Whole Note Silence

Quarter Note Sound

Quarter Note Silence

Eighth Note Sound

Eighth Note Silence

Sixteenth Note Sound

Sixteenth Note Silence

Thirty-Second Note Sound

Thirty-Second Note Silence

Sixty-Fourth Note Sound

Sixty-Fourth Note Silence

One Hundred-Twenty-Eighth
Note Sound

One Hundred-Twenty-Eighth
Note Silence

For every musical notation of the duration of sound, there is
an equal notation for the duration of silence.

music, as powerful as the surrounding notes," but also "a critical life skill." The ability to silence the inner voice creates the conditions for truly hearing the voices of others. It also better enables a clearer perception of what is happening in the moment. Hancock affirmed in his talks that his Buddhist practice deepened his understanding of these capabilities. He's an example of how musicians who are trained to be sensitive to both sound and silence can apply that skill to increase their compassion, insight, and mindfulness in all aspects of life.

_____

The ability to silence the inner voice creates the conditions for truly hearing the voices of others.

_____

As significant as silence is to music, in meditation a primary motivation is to achieve silence of the mind. We practice stilling the body and quieting the mind from the constant agitation of distractions and preoccupations. Eventually we can find ourselves in a state of silent awareness, where the constant buzzing of thoughts relaxes into stillness. In our environment we hear the space from which sounds emerge and the space to which they return. It is that special state of consciousness that we've been primed for through our attunement to the interplay between sound and silence in music. The mind is stable and unclouded, allowing whatever happens within our sphere of experience to be known peacefully. In that profound stillness it's possible to break through to what some have described as going beyond sound and silence to the source of perception and nonperception itself.

Miles and Herbie are not the only musicians who have made the use of silence a touchstone in their compositions. In the next section we will discuss composers who design their compositions as nonverbal guided meditations on the nature of sound and silence, leading the audience to a transformation in their consciousness.

COMPOSERS OF SILENCE AND
THE BEAUTIFUL MIND

When the Dadaist Marcel Duchamp plucked an industrial uri-
nal out of a warehouse, signed it, and titled it *Fountain*, he was
drilling through the wall separating art from life. Duchamp is
credited with being one of the first to expose the role of cul-
turally conditioned perception in tipping the balance between
beauty and plainness. And if everyday objects could be art, then
ordinary sounds could be music. In fact, the futurist composer
Luigi Russolo had already demonstrated in *The Art of Noises* that
listening in the right way could transform ordinary noises into a
powerful musical experience.

From these beginnings in Dadaism and futurism to the most
contemporary movements of minimalism and *Wandelweiser,* artists have been channeling our attention toward the process of
perception itself as much as toward the objects of perception.
The most seminal musical artist in this movement highlighting
the interdependence of the observer with the observed, noise
with music, sound with silence, and "art without works of art" is
the composer John Cage.

If everyday objects could be art,
then ordinary sounds could be music.

In his most famous piece, *4'33"*, Cage leads the audience in a nonverbal guided meditation on the nature of attentive listening and the presence of sound and silence. It's usually performed by a pianist sitting stiffly at the piano, without playing, for 4 minutes and 33 seconds. In that ostensible silence, the audience nevertheless continues to hear things: innumerable ambient sounds such as shuffling, coughing, air conditioning, breathing, and so on. Cage draws the audience's attention to the process of listening itself but without a definite object. He is creating a state of awareness in the audience, so that they can be mindful of what they are experiencing at the moment. They are brought closer to the realization that absolute silence, which is beyond physical sound and silence, can only be realized through a special state of consciousness. Cage's promotion of the nonduality of art and life, silence and "the music of the world," set in motion a revolution in art and music that is still ongoing.*

From the second half of the twentieth century until now, Western artists and composers have been playing with this notion that the perceiver is as vital a part of the artistic process as the perceived. These creators demonstrate that art—like everything else—ultimately takes place in the mind. Painting, for example, is an interaction that travels "off the wall" and into our consciousness. For icons of pop art and performance art alike, the state of mind of the spectator *is* the work of art. Just

---

* Cage's influence can be found in innumerable artistic productions: in the pop art of Jasper Johns and Robert Rauschenberg; in the video art of Bruce Nauman and Nam June Paik; and in the conceptual and performance art of Yoko Ono and Marina Abramović, to name a few.

as in deep meditative states there is no separation between the subject and the object, the knower and the known, foreground and background, relative and absolute, so in these new forms of art performer and audience, onlooker and art object, are one integrated experience.

For Cage, Russolo, and their many modern descendants, musical composition is as much about deepening the audiences' awareness of the soundscape it inhabits from minute to minute as it is about creating a defined musical work. These composers seek to heighten the awareness of phenomena as they arise in the listener's sonic environment, whether by "indeterminate" chance or by design. Their compositions break down the barriers between performer and listener, inviting the audiences' participation in active and mindful listening to animate the poetics of their compositions.

A new school of composition that is based on the art of deep listening is known as Wandelweiser. Musicians associated with Wandelweiser are highly attuned to the inseparable connectivity between the poles of silence and sound and to the way in which music can shape our experience of time and space. *The New Yorker* music critic Alex Ross writes that Wandelweiser "is not so much a style as a life style." The Wandelweiser composer Michael Pisaro, explaining the momentous influence of John Cage on his fellow musicians, notes that *4'33"* "created new possibilities for the combination (and understanding) of sound and silence. Put simply, silence was a material and a disturbance of material at the same time." The aftereffects of a Wandelweiser concert are described as a state of deep, peaceful concentration and a feeling of contentment that seems to purify the senses while cultivating a new appreciation for the vast soundscape and the whole field of experience. Ring a bell?

There are many other individual examples of mindful composers. The acclaimed composer Pauline Oliveros dedicated her professional life to cultivating the art of deep listening in the public at large. She even asserted that she preferred engaging with nonmusicians in her compositions that require intensive audience participation. Her music plays as guided meditations focused on heightening the audience members' awareness of their sonic environment. With her Deep Listening Band and intricate text scores like the *Sonic Meditations*, her work encourages a level of concentration that yields a fresh, receptive appreciation for sound and its relation to all of life.

Just as artful listening can transcend the bounds of ordinary awareness, a silent meditation can transform into a moment of art.

From the minimalist composer La Monte Young dragging a chair and table across the floor in performance to the ensemble So Percussion performing the minimalist composer Steve Reich's *Music for Pieces of Wood* in a hardware store, the adventurous continue to break silence and sound barriers, continually expanding the universe of mindful composition and deep listening. These composers of silence and the beautiful mind show us how appreciating works of meditative art can enhance appreciation of mindfulness practice, and vice versa. Just as artful listening can transcend the bounds of ordinary awareness, a silent meditation can transform into a moment of art.

THE SONG WRITES YOU

"Somedays the song writes you."—**Guy Clark**

There is an anecdote about the legendary Shunryu Suzuki. He is in a dialogue, or *dokusan*, with a student. They are discussing the student's practice of Zen meditation known as zazen. The student is very excited because he has overcome a big obstacle in his practice. Up until now meditation has been very difficult for many years. Finally, he feels he has broken through. He tells Suzuki with great enthusiasm that he can now do zazen with profound success. But his teacher responds with irritation: "Never think that *you* are sitting zazen . . . zazen is sitting zazen."

You allow the music to move through you

*out into the world. You **are** the music;*

we can't say who is playing whom.

Between the instrument and the instrumentalist there is no block. As Keith Richards said, the riff "plays you." When you are truly absorbed in the moment-to-moment energy stream of pure awareness, it's not something that *you* yourself are *doing*. Zazen is doing zazen. When playing music, you let go of all your closely held preoccupations to totally immerse yourself in the soundscape. Meditation is similar in that way to the artist being attuned to the inspiration that creates the art. The meditator, like the artist, suspends the conceptual walls of the ego shell to receive the waves of the universal self as they move through you and guide your hands on the keyboard. You allow the music to move through you out into the world. You *are* the music; we can't say who is playing whom.

Many of the exercises that we've been practicing have interwoven tonal, harmonic, or rhythmic patterns into traditional meditation modalities. When meditation techniques are imbued with musical features that sound only within our consciousness, it can be a process both of transcendent awareness and spontaneous creativity. In the tradition of Cage, Oliveros, and the other composers of silence, we are creating musical works that have inherent value both as music and as paths to meditative mindfulness. As we compose a kind of internal music we are also composing ourselves. So many musicians, celebrated and uncelebrated, have found it searingly painful when the music stops and the normal challenges of life resume. With these practices, the barriers between music and life splinter just like all the other boundaries that divide self from other, mind from body, art from life. The diverse currents all merge like waves on an endless stream; guitarist and riff, performer and audience, the knower and the known, the singer and the song.

Bonus Tracks

MORE MODES OF MINDFULNESS TRAINING

Once you've mastered the basic tonal breath methods explained in previous chapters, it might be fun for the more musically adventurous to experiment with the methods that follow. These techniques presume that the meditator has experience practicing some of the fundamental tonal methods as well as a familiarity with the concept of musical intervals. The instructions are gentle guidelines meant to suggest a framework for further improvisation, so that the practitioner at once creates or "freestyles" a spontaneous composition and eases into a concentrative state of deep absorption.

Tonal Breath
Meditations

Sequencing Tones

Here's a suggestion for one variation of a tonal pattern that uses the interval of a minor third descending to the tonic, or root note, on the inhalation, and the fourth interval descending to the tonic on the exhalation. The music would be heard as the slow sequence of two tones moving simultaneously with the inhalation, and the next two tones in sync with the exhalation. For example:

Inhalation: E♭ (half note duration/2 beats) ⟶ middle C (half note duration)

Exhalation: F (half note duration/2 beats) ⟶ middle C (half note duration)

You can experiment with an ascending sequence in place of the descending one. You may even add a third note to the pattern. And of course, you can use any combination of intervals that happen to occur to you at the moment. As always, any pitches you hear are the perfect pitches—and that's why you're hearing them.

You can also speed up the sequence so that it repeats. The pattern can sound like a variation of a Philip Glass/Steve Reich–style four-note minimalist ostinato (a repetitive sequence) where the notes are expressed as eighth or quarter notes instead of whole or half notes (sixteenth notes would be too fast). Be aware, though, that these methods are risky, because they can easily devolve into critical appraisal, which can sidetrack us from the relaxed, enhanced awareness we are cultivating. When in doubt, keep it simple.

Alternating Tonal and Nontonal Breathing

As you pick up various techniques of tonal breathing, you can experiment with balancing cycles of tonal breathing with nontonal breathing. After a cycle of tonal breathing, listen deeply to your normal breathing, without adding any tonal or harmonic layers. Try to breathe as softly and gently as possible while keeping the breath audible. This will invite your mind to listen and focus carefully, sharpening your ears' awareness—a result of listening deeply in both meditation and musical practice.

Sometimes you will still hear a tone or chord reverberating in your mind when you want to progress to a silent phase. Direct your attention to the sound of your breathing and the respiratory movements of your body. Listen carefully to the breath and peripherally to any ambient sounds that may emerge. After a while the "tail" of the note left over from your tonal breathing will totally decay, and it will be replaced in your awareness with the sound of your breath. Listen closely during the rests between breaths. Eventually the silence will come through.

Trichord Meditation: Arpeggiation

"If our hearts were as pure, as chaste, and as snowy as Pythagoras' was, our ears would resound and be filled with that supremely lovely music of the wheeling stars."—**John Milton**

TRICHORD MEDITATION IS A SERIES of meditations made up of Pythagorean intervals. These modalities are more involved and a bit more musically complex than most other methods in this book. They may offer the kind of challenge that will keep a restless musical mind properly focused. For those with a decent grasp of harmony they are really quite simple and fun once you get the idea. Ultimately, they are just another series of techniques among many others.

The Greek philosopher Pythagoras believed that there are three intervals basic to all creation and therefore most pleasing to the human ear: the fourth, the fifth, and the octave. The Pythagoreans believed that these were the only harmonious intervals in music; since these intervals represent the mathematical ratios upon which the physical bodies, energy, and the entire cosmos depend, they are transcendent and calming to the human soul. Channeling this mode can seem daunting and does require some technical facility, but as with any meditation practice it can be learned over time.

Sit in a classic meditation posture, with a relaxed body. When you inhale, generate a tone in your mind's ear. This will be your tonic. (The dual meaning of the term *tonic*—as a balm or soothing agent—is quite appealing for our purposes.) Hold the tone as you inhale and count to seven. After the count hold your breath and "rest" for as long as it feels comfortable. Then exhale hearing the same tone and also counting until seven. At the end of the exhalation rest again for as long as it feels natural.

You may think of it as holding or playing the tonic note in 7/4 time, if that is something that occurs to you as you do this meditation. It's important to remember that the tempo is completely flexible; you may think of it as eternally rubato. The tempo may change in the middle of the "bar" (if each individual inhalation is one bar, and each individual exhalation another bar). It may change in the middle of a note. Your concentration should be on the breath, the note, and the count. The tempo of the count doesn't matter but will gradually slow down as your breathing becomes deeper. The rhythm of the breath as it evolves in your meditation is not tied to a metronome or any measurement of time that the practical, analytical mind needs to grasp. The rhythm is tied to whatever is happening at the present moment.

If we think of each individual inhalation as one bar, and each individual exhalation as a bar, then we are holding the root/tonic note for two bars or one breath. With the next breath, hear a tone a third above the tonic. As with the tonic, listen to that tone both in the inhalation and during the exhalation. Remember to hold your breath and rest at the end of the bar, both at the end of the inhalation and at the end of the exhalation. The timing of the rest is completely improvised and flexible. You may hear the note that you are holding taper off into silence, or you may hear silence itself. Listen carefully to whatever arises.

With the next breath you will hear the fifth above the tonic. The procedure for holding the note for a seven count for each bar and resting at the end of the bar is the same for this note as it is for the other two notes. Remember that the tempo within a bar is not set and can slow down or speed up at will. The important thing is to hold the note for the count, to focus on the breathing and the note, and to listen deeply during the rest at the end of the bar. For this practice a 1, 3, 5 progression or major or minor fifth triad is a natural harmonic experience.

Historically, too, the major fifth has been understood as a root vibration at the source of the cosmos as well as having special divine power. This power of the fifth was intuitive to the Greeks, and Pythagoras layered his mathematical analysis of intervals over this esthetic preference. So using the fifth in whatever triad you express during your meditation will help bring about a sense of tranquility and equanimity, making it an especially good way to begin a trichord meditation. Quieting our analytical, discriminating mind and nurturing our intuitive intelligence is key to our practice. Naturally, the triad that you hear internally can be made of any three notes that the moment chooses. Ultimately the important thing is to follow the basic principles of this trichord meditation whether you incorporate the fifth or not.

At first you will be holding the seven count on one note for one bar. You can slow the count down to a six-, five-, or four-count per bar if you wish. It's important to sync the count with your breathing, no matter what the number is. The count and the tone both help to focus the mind and maintain the concentration on the breath.

Cycle through this method of expressing the triad until you are ready for a change. The next stage will be to give silent tones to the three notes of the triad (voicelessly of course) within one bar. So space out hearing the three notes, starting with the tonic and then move up to the next note, then the next. They should fill the space of one inhalation, so there's a bit of stretching involved as well. Remember to pause at the top of the inhalation. Then during the exhalation, hear the three notes again, voiced beginning with the tonic and then moving up the scale. The notes are expressed individually at a relatively slow pace within the bar, so that they don't necessarily feel like an arpeggiation but a progression of notes. If you like, you can hold the final note of the inhalation through the entire exhalation.

As you meditate, voice the three notes within the bar at a faster rate, as if you were arpeggiating. At the end of one arpeggiation, hold the last tone in your consciousness until the end of the bar. During the rest bar, listen to the tone or tones taper off into silence. As with all the other methods, this sequence is repeated during each inhalation and each exhalation, as is the rest bar in between.

Now hasten the arpeggio so that you are expressing the three notes almost as a strummed chord. If you want to strum them with a pick at a pace so that each individual note can still be heard, then voice the chord that way. If you feel like strumming the chord so the notes blend and only the chord is heard, do that. Most people find that option more difficult, so it's a matter of choice, not necessity. The important matter is to hear the triad however you can and hold it for a bar, rest, then hold it again for another bar.

The Pythagorean Intervals

AS WE SAW, THE PYTHAGOREAN school held that there are certain intervals that are at the base of all phenomena and therefore the most pleasing to the human ear and soul. Each contains two opposing principles—such as male/female, heat/cold, light/dark, justice/injustice, good/evil—and their unification in a sequence of three tones represents the transcendent unitary principle of the cosmos. Thus in music, we have a demonstration of the oneness that is the true nature of the universe. The three main series of intervals:

1-4-5

1-5-8

1-4-8

As a meditation technique, the simplest to start with is the 1-4-5 sequence. Use this sequence in the manner explained in the previous chapter on trichord meditation. First you express each note separately while counting and attending to the breath for two bars: one complete inhalation plus one exhalation (one bar each). Start with the root, working your way up to the four and then the five.

You can visualize the sequence as a triangle while you progress through it: One side of the base is the root (one), the other side of the base is the second note (in this case the fourth), and the apex is the highest note (the fifth). In music, and in meditation, we often progress from the root and then work our way up (only to end up at the root again).

In this way, we tap into the ultimate harmony inherent in everything, and the unitary principle that is the ground of all being.

Strumming the Mind-Body Guitar

ONCE YOU'VE PASSED THROUGH THE slower trichords and arpeggiations, you may begin sounding the triad in your mind. You can sound the triad as if you were strumming a guitar chord and with each strum hit a quarter-note count. Synchronize the count with your breathing, so that again one inhalation is one bar, its accompanying exhalation also one bar.

Breathe slowly enough to maintain a four count so that you are sounding four quarter-note expressions of the triad with each inhalation and each exhalation. Remember you are only listening to the triad you have been working with, not layering in any other chords or notes.

Just as the triad unifies different tones into one chord, it simultaneously unifies different energies within your mind-body.

Different energies are always vibrating at various frequencies within you. When sounding the triad in your mind you are uniting these various energies and frequencies into one vibration, one unitary frequency. You can visualize this overarching frequency as white light. Just as white light contains all the frequencies of visible light and invisible light (ultraviolet, X-rays, and so on), your triad contains all the frequencies within your mind-body. The triad meditation theoretically unifies the multitude of frequency/energies within your mind and body into one chord, just as white light unifies a multitude of energies into one. As you strum your mind-body guitar, the triad of unified vibrations resounds throughout all creation. Visualize this as if you are in effect hearing in your consciousness the white light that is the true essence of your mind-body.

Ultimately as you sit with your triad of infinite light, you begin to doubt whether it is really you or your concept of you that is sounding the triad. Are you the one generating the chord you are experiencing, or is it the whole of existence that is generating the chord?

Ultimately as you sit with your triad of infinite light, you begin to doubt whether it is really you or your concept of you that is sounding the triad.

TONAL BREATH COUNTING: FAQ

How long should the notes last when counting?

The tones being sung with every number do not have a fixed length. The durations of the tones are contingent on the timing of the breath. The first tone lasts as long as the inhalation, and the following tone or tones as long as the exhalation. So you may think of the notes as legato in how they are sustained. Again the tempo always varies with the contingencies of the moment. The tempo can change from one number to the next.

What notes can I use?

For ease of illustration within some of the techniques, I've used middle C (do) and whole or half tones above or below; e.g., D and B (re, ti). But this is primarily a suggestion and by no means a rule. You can use any root tone that your mind settles on at the moment. It's not important what tones you use, so long as the notes intuitively feel right and are easy to sing in your mind. Whatever tones you spontaneously land on are always the natural and ideal tones for those moments.

What intervals can I use?

There are schools of meditation that proclaim that an expert needs to provide you with your own personal mantra. In the tonal breath method you are your own expert. You find the tones and intervals that work for you and feel right at the moment. Most people find that hewing to one tone with a few close intervals gets them the furthest. But there may be times when you may hear more complex tones and intervals. There is no right or wrong tone or interval or groups of tones. As long as you focus on counting the breath and the breath-holding periods, it's all good. Whatever music works for you in keeping your concentration "steady rollin'" is the right music. You are the best provider of your own personal mantra.

How important is holding the breath after the inhalations and holding the contraction of the abdomen after the exhalation?

In *A Guide to Zen*, Katsuki Sekida instructs: "Exhale as much air as possible and then remain without breathing for a considerable period." This technique of exhaling and holding of the contraction after exhalation is called *susokkan*. He explains: The more you contract the respiratory muscles during exhalation to force as much air as possible out of the lungs and then hold the contraction of the respiratory muscles, "the more quickly you will attain samadhi [total absorption in concentration] and the deeper it will be."

You may find that it is difficult to both hold your breath after inhalation and hold the contraction after exhalation. Both types of holding the breath are beneficial. Just play it by inner ear as far as how long you want to hold either one, or which technique you want to emphasize. The resonant silence, or rest sections, are also very useful, because they allow you to catch your breath. Once you have done a few rest patterns your momentum will be restored, and you can go back to the regular breath counting.

Coda: A Still Small Voice

WE SOMETIMES THINK OF THE God of the Bible as appearing in a great commotion of sound and fury, lightning and thunder on top of a mountain. But in 1 Kings 19, where we meet the prophet Elijah searching for God out of the depths of despair, we hear a different story.

When God appears to Elijah it is not in sound and fury, fire and earthquake, but rather in a "still small voice." The narrative is very specific in emphasizing the difference between titanic displays of cataclysmic activity and God's quiet stillness. Rather than manifesting in the midst of loud and powerful sounds, God appears in a small voice, closer to silence. "And behold, the Lord passed by, and a great and strong wind rent the mountains . . . but the Lord was *not* in the wind; and after the wind an earthquake; but the Lord was *not* in the earthquake; and after the earthquake a fire; but the Lord was *not* in the fire; and after the fire a *still small voice*. And it was so, when Elijah heard it, that he wrapped his face in the mantle, and went out" (verses 11 to 13, emphasis mine).

In the stillness of meditation, that's a sound we could be listening for.

Acknowledgments

I owe the following people a huge debt of gratitude:

Stephany Evans, my literary agent, for her early, full-throated support and steadfastness; my editor, Jennifer Kurdyla, for instantly getting what I was trying to accomplish and putting so much of her heart, yoga, keen intellect, and incandescent energy into improving the book; Professor Ken Lopez, a true mentor, for cajoling and strong-arming me into teaching this subject; Joel Schwartz, PhD, the first reader and fellow high schooler Zen Center traveler for his expert and necessary critiques and suggestions; Chuck Crisafulli for his peerless tips and skilled journalistic perspective; Clyde Lieberman for sharing his original approach to staying cool and judicious under fire.

For their invaluable guidance, contributions, and hearty encouragement, I owe the brilliant consiglieri Gary Stiffelman, Esq., Amram Shapiro, Steve Winogradsky, Dr. Sandford Pepper, Dave "Hard Drive" Pensado, Peter Scaturro and Peter

DiCecco; the multi-talented Hannah Bowers and Christina Higa for assistance with an array of literary duties; my discerning publishers Matthew Lore and Peter Burri; Dr. Michael Quick and Varun Soni, PhD, for their unflagging and visionary support of mindfulness initiatives at USC; Professor Allen Weiss for helping me teach the subject from the beginning and for schooling me in some user-friendly and impactful ways of applying mindfulness; inspirational teachers Amy Spies, Dr. Glenn Fox, and JoAnna Hardy for adding their singular perspectives in class; Kendrick Lamar, thank you for approving the lyric; Ezra Byda and Elizabeth Hamilton of The Zen Center of San Diego, who provide a welcoming home and transcendent experience for meditators; Thich Nhat Hanh for his miraculous gifts as a teacher, writer, and founder of Deer Park Monastery.

My children, Elijah and Caroline, for their brutal forthrightness in appraising all my theories; interfaith innovator Clifford Wolf; my parents, Jacques and Charlotte Wolf, for not only starting me on the path but shining a light along the way. And I am most grateful to my wife, Roz, for her irrational fealty, limitless understanding, and wisdom, as well as her grasp of relativistic reality, without which I would still be teetering on a ladder trying to change a bulb while having a panic attack.

Text Credits

Epigraph: from *Seeds of Wisdom: Based on Personal Encounters with the Rebbe, Rabbi Menachem M. Schneerson*, by Mendel Kalmenson, courtesy of Jewish Educational Media.

Page 13: from *Words Without Music*, by Philip Glass, courtesy of Liveright, an imprint of W. W. Norton & Company, Inc.

Page 21: Words and Music by KENDRICK LAMAR and
MATHIEU RAKOTOZAFY
Copyright © 2016 TOP DAWG MUSIC, HARD WORKING
BLACK FOLKS, INC.,
WB MUSIC CORP and COPYRIGHT CONTROL
All Rights on behalf of Itself TOP DAWG MUSIC and HARD
WORKING BLACK FOLKS, INC.
Administered by WB MUSIC CORP.
All Rights Reserved
Used By Permission of ALFRED MUSIC

Page 105: from "The Pleasures of Peace" in *The Collected Poems of Kenneth Koch*, by Kenneth Koch, courtesy of Knopf, an imprint of Penguin Random House, LLC.

Suggested Reading

Meditation and Mindfulness

Aurelius, Marcus. *Meditations*. New York: Clydesdale Press, 2018.

Batchelor, Stephen. *Buddhism Without Beliefs: A Contemporary Guide to Awakening*. New York: Riverhead, 1997.

Blyth, R. H. *Zen and Zen Classics*. New York: Vintage Books, 1978.

Chödrön, Pema. *How to Meditate: A Practical Guide to Making Friends with Your Mind*. Boulder: Sounds True, 2013.

Dass, Ram. *Journey of Awakening: A Meditator's Guidebook*. Toronto: Bantam, 1978.

Epstein, Mark. *Thoughts Without a Thinker: Psychotherapy from a Buddhist Perspective*. New York: Basic Books, 1995.

Goldstein, Joseph, and Jack Kornfield. *Seeking the Heart of Wisdom: The Path of Insight Meditation*. Boston: Shambhala, 1987.

Goleman, Daniel. *The Meditative Mind: The Varieties of Meditative Experience*. Los Angeles: Tarcher, 1988.

Hanh, Thich Nhat. *Breathe! You Are Alive: Sutra on the Full Awareness of Breathing*. Berkeley: Parallax, 1990.

———. *The Miracle of Mindfulness: An Introduction to the Practice of Meditation*. Boston: Beacon, 1999.

Harris, Dan. *10% Happier: How I Tamed the Voice in My Head, Reduced Stress Without Losing My Edge, and Found Self-Help That Actually Works—A True Story*. New York: It Books, 2014.

Harris, Sam. *Waking Up: A Guide to Spirituality Without Religion*. New York: Simon & Schuster, 2015.

Kabat-Zinn, Jon. *Wherever You Go, There You Are: Mindfulness Meditation in Everyday Life*. New York: Hyperion, 1994.

Kaplan, Aryeh. *Meditation and Kabbalah*. Newburyport: Weiser, 1989.

Loori, John Daido. *The Zen of Creativity: Cultivating Your Artistic Life*. New York: Ballantine, 2004.

Maharshi, Ramana. *Be As You Are: The Teachings of Sri Ramana Maharshi*. London: Arkana, 1985.

Mipham, Sakyong. *Turning the Mind Into an Ally*. New York: Riverhead, 2003.

Shrobe, Richard. *Elegant Failure: A Guide to Zen Koans*. Berkeley: Rodmell, 2010.

Suzuki, Daisetz Teitaro. *Zen Buddhism: Selected Writings of D. T. Suzuki*. New York: Doubleday, 1956.

Tarrant, John. *Bring Me the Rhinoceros: And Other Zen Koans That Will Save Your Life*. Boston: Shambhala, 2008.

Wallace, Alan B. *Choosing Reality: A Contemplative View of Physics and the Mind.* Boulder: New Science Library, 1989.

Watts, Alan. *The Wisdom of Insecurity: A Message for an Age of Anxiety.* New York: Pantheon, 1951.

Wu, John C. H. *The Golden Age of Zen: The Classic Work on the Foundation of Zen Philosophy.* New York: Image, 1996.

Yamada, Koun. *The Gateless Gate: The Classic Book of Zen Koans.* Somerville: Wisdom Publications, 2004.

Music

Glass, Philip. *Words Without Music: A Memoir.* New York: Liveright, 2015.

Hancock, Herbie, and Lisa Dickey. *Herbie Hancock: Possibilities.* New York: Viking, 2014.

Larson, Kay. *Where the Heart Beats: John Cage, Zen Buddhism, and the Inner Life of Artists.* New York: Penguin, 2012.

Mercer, Michelle. *Footprints: The Life and Work of Wayne Shorter.* New York: TarcherPerigee, 2007.

Oliveros, Pauline. *Deep Listening: A Composer's Sound Practice.* Bloomington: iUniverse, Inc., 2005.

Richards, Keith. *Life.* New York: Little, Brown, 2010.

Ross, Alex. "The Composers of Quiet." *The New Yorker,* September 5, 2016.

Springsteen, Bruce. *Born to Run.* New York: Simon & Schuster, 2016.

About the Author

RICHARD WOLF is an Emmy Award–winning composer, multi-platinum-selling music producer, and professor at the University of Southern California's Thornton School of Music, where he teaches classes on music and mindfulness. As a producer/remixer/songwriter/composer, Wolf worked on projects with Prince, Bell Biv DeVoe, Freddie Mercury, MC Lyte, and Coolio, and has been contributing to the soundtracks for hundreds of films and television episodes, including twelve seasons of the worldwide hit, *NCIS*. He started practicing Zen meditation when he was a teenager.

richardwolf.net